Strategies for
Successful
Classroom
Management

To Laura
Because I knew you, I have been changed for good . . .
                                        —Brian Mendler

To my loving grandchildren
Yocheved Chana, Betzalel Ze'ev, Noa Bareket,
Eli Seth, Ryan Joseph, Megan Alana, and
Chana Rivka. You are the joy of my life.
                                        —Rick Curwin

To my grandchildren
Caleb and Ava for making me feel young again.
Your innocence and inquisitiveness reminds me of how
natural it is to want to learn and love. I adore you both.
                                        —Allen Mendler

Strategies for Successful Classroom Management

Helping Students Succeed Without Losing Your Dignity or Sanity

Brian D. Mendler   Richard L. Curwin   Allen N. Mendler

CORWIN PRESS
A SAGE Company
Thousand Oaks, CA 91320

For information:

Corwin Press
A SAGE Company
2455 Teller Road
Thousand Oaks,
    California 91320
www.corwinpress.com

SAGE Ltd.
1 Oliver's Yard
55 City Road
London EC1Y 1SP
United Kingdom

SAGE India Pvt. Ltd.
B 1/I 1 Mohan Cooperative
    Industrial Area
Mathura Road,
    New Delhi 110 044
India

SAGE Asia-Pacific Pte. Ltd.
33 Pekin Street #02-01
Far East Square
Singapore 048763

Printed in the United States of America.

Library of Congress Cataloging-in-Publication Data

Mendler, Brian.
Strategies for successful classroom management: helping students succeed without losing your dignity or sanity/Brian Mendler, Richard L. Curwin, Allen N. Mendler.
    p. cm.
Includes bibliographical references and index.
ISBN 978-1-4129-3783-2 (cloth)
ISBN 978-1-4129-3784-9 (pbk.)
    1. School discipline. 2. Behavior modification. 3. Classroom management.
I. Curwin, Richard L., 1944- II. Mendler, Allen N. III. Title.

LB3012.M462 2008
371.102′4—dc22   2007036306

This book is printed on acid-free paper.

07 08 09 10 11   10 9 8 7 6 5 4 3 2 1

Acquisitions Editor:	Jessica Allan
Editorial Assistant:	Joanna Coelho
Production Editor:	Veronica Stapleton
Copy Editor:	Alison Hope
Typesetter:	C&M Digitals (P) Ltd.
Proofreader:	Kristin Bergstad
Indexer:	Kirsten Kite
Cover Designer:	Russ Nemec
Graphic Designer:	Scott Van Atta

Contents

Acknowledgments

I would like to begin by thanking my dad, mentor, and friend, Allen Mendler. Dad, you have spent your life dedicated to making the world a better place for children. Thanks for trusting me to carry on the *Discipline With Dignity* message and for being the best father a guy could have.

To Rick Curwin, an amazing teacher, mentor, and friend: Thanks for creating the best classroom management program in the world, and thanks for allowing me to carry it forward.

Mom, you are a wonderful parent, educator, and friend. I love you.

Jason, your hard work, dedication, and focus are traits that I admire. Thanks for your support, friendship, and love. You are an amazing human being and I am proud to be your brother. Lisa, you are smart, kind, caring, and beautiful. I love you.

Ticia, I admire and respect you so much. My brother is lucky to have you as his wife and I am lucky to have you as a sister-in-law and friend. Thanks for your dedication to Jason, Caleb, Ava, and Belly.

To my students, many of whom are mentioned by name in this book, including AJ, Anthony, Ashley, Ben, Dan, Jenna, Joe, Kyle, Liz, Mike, Russell, and all others I had the pleasure of working with: I didn't know how to teach until I met you.

Ms. Farrell, you are an amazing person, educator, friend, and colleague. Thanks for your unrelenting support and dedication. You made my life and the lives of our students better. I will always be grateful.

Rush-Henrietta and Wheatland-Chili had the guts to take a chance on a young, energetic, and occasionally opinionated teacher. Jim Decamp and Kerry Dempsey taught me so much. Thanks to each of you.

To Mike and Bud at St. John Fisher College, thanks for your dedication to me. I am proud to teach at such a fine institution.

A special thanks to Becky Zelesnikar and her fourth graders at Longridge Elementary for allowing me to be a part of their class this summer.

To my Monday and Tuesday night support groups: None of this book was possible without my meetings. I learned to be honest, responsible, and committed. You taught me that truth is most important, even though it is not always easy. Kevin, Chuck, Connie, Bruno, Sandy, Bill, and anyone else brave enough to come, helped change my life. "Keep coming back. It works if you work it so work it. You're worth it."

To my "little brother" Victor and the Big Brothers Big Sisters program: Vic, you are a wonderful part of my life. I am proud to be your friend, mentor, and brother.

—Brian Mendler

This project would not have happened without the work of our wonderful staff at the Teacher Learning Center and Discipline Associates: Jon, Allison, Jamie, Jennifer, and Heidi. In addition, we are extremely fortunate to have an outstanding group of associates that support, share, and grow our work with educators throughout the country: Willeta Corbett, Jerry Evanski, Mary Beth Hewitt, Donald Price, Colleen and David Zawadzki, and Cynthia Glenn.

Thanks to Scott Pecore for your friendship, advice, support, and consultation.

To Alison Hope, Veronica Stapleton, and all the fine people at Corwin Press: Thank you so much for your dedication, patience, and support. We are so grateful for your hard work and professionalism.

Finally, to all dedicated teachers for the daily effort and persistence it takes to make differences in the lives of your students: We thank you on their behalf.

—Brian, Rick, and Allen

In addition, the contributions of the following reviewers are gratefully acknowledged:

Kathryn Fitzgerald Abels, MSW
EC Resource Teacher
Charlotte Mecklenberg Schools
Charlotte, NC

Deborah Alexander-Davis, EdD
Educational Consultant, Adjunct Professor, Research
    Associate, Retired Elementary Principal
    2004 Tennessee Principal of the Year
Kingston, TN

Judy Brunner
Author and Consultant
Edu-Safe LLC
Springfield, MO

Catherine Kilfoyle Duffy
English Department Chairperson
Three Village Central School District
Stony Brook, NY

Sheila Fisher
Principal
Maria Weston Chapman Middle School
East Weymouth, MA

Barbara K. Given, PhD
Director, Adolescent and Adult Learning Research
    Center, Krasnow Institute for Advanced Study, and
    Director, Center for Honoring Individual Learning
    Diversity, an International Learning Styles Center
George Mason University
Fairfax, VA

Debra Las
ISD #535, Rochester Public Schools
Rochester, MN

Diane P. Smith
School Counselor
Port Allegany, PA

Stephen Valentine
English Department Chair
Montclair Kimberley Academy
Montclair, NJ

About the Authors

 **Brian D. Mendler** is a certified elementary and special education teacher with extensive experience working with students who have challenging behaviors in general education, self-contained, and inclusion settings. As an adjunct professor at St. John Fisher College in Rochester, NY, he teaches behavior management and introduction to special education. In addition, he provides staff development training for K–12 educators and youth service workers throughout North America with the focus on how to be successful with students who have moderate to severe behavior difficulties. Mr. Mendler's recent publication, *Tips 4 Teachers,* is an easy-to-read book for educators that offers specific, practical strategies from the *Discipline With Dignity* approach. Mr. Mendler is a contributor to the book *Just in Time: Powerful Strategies to Promote Positive Behavior,* published with Dr. Allen Mendler, and coauthor of numerous publications, including *Discipline With Dignity.* That publication provides practical, in-depth suggestions for teachers that offer solutions to problems with discipline and motivation.

While completing his master's degree at D'Youville College in Buffalo, NY, Mr. Mendler began volunteering in the Big Brothers Big Sisters program. He has been passionately involved with this program, and his "little" brother, Victor, since that time. He also works with Special Olympics, helping out in their track and field and softball programs. Mr. Mendler currently lives in Rochester, NY.

Richard L. Curwin is an award-winning instructor, author, and educational consultant. His philosophy on discipline, behavior, and classroom management is one of the most widely used in the world. He is coauthor of the national best-selling book *Discipline With Dignity*, which offers educators a plethora of strategies on behavior and classroom management. Dr. Curwin has also written or cowritten many other publications, including *Discipline With Dignity for Challenging Youth*, *Rediscovering Hope: Our Greatest Teaching Strategy*, and *Making Good Choices*.

His seminars and training sessions offer educators ready-to-use strategies with objectives, materials, language, and examples—all designed to encourage students to accept responsibility for their own behavior. Dr. Curwin believes that mistakes can become opportunities for learning, and that they provide teachers a chance to teach respect and self-discipline. His articles have appeared in *Educational Leadership*, *Reclaiming Children and Youth*, and *Instructor, Parenting,* and *Learning*, all of which are highly acclaimed educational resources.

He is a leader in the fields of discipline, behavior, and classroom management. He is in high demand as a speaker in America and internationally. His strategies and techniques are used in Belgium, Germany, Japan, Singapore, and Israel. He was a recipient of the coveted Crazy Horse Award for having made outstanding contributions to discouraged youth.

Curwin has three children and five grandchildren. He makes his home in San Francisco, CA.

Dr. Allen N. Mendler is an educator, school psychologist, behavior and classroom management expert, and parent of three children.

He has worked extensively with children of all ages in regular education and special education settings. He has consulted at many schools on the topics of discipline, behavior, and classroom management. He has also consulted at day and residential centers, and has done extensive work with youth in juvenile detention.

Dr. Mendler's emphasis is on developing effective frameworks and strategies for educators to manage behavior and classrooms. He is an expert at helping youth professionals, teachers, administrators, and parents help youth who have difficulties achieving success.

As one of the internationally acclaimed authors of the book *Discipline With Dignity*, Dr. Mendler has given many workshops and seminars to professionals and parents. His behavior management philosophy is highly acclaimed, and Dr. Mendler is in demand as a motivational speaker and trainer by schools all over the world.

He is the author or coauthor of many books, including *What Do I Do When?*; *Power Struggles: Successful Techniques for Educators*; *Motivating Students Who Don't Care*; *Connecting With Students*; and *Discipline With Dignity for Challenging Youth*. Dr. Mendler's most recent book, *Just in Time*, provides practical easy-to-read tips and specific methods for preventing discipline problems. His articles have appeared in many highly acclaimed journals, including *Educational Leadership*, *Kappan*, *Learning*, *Reclaiming Children and Youth*, and *Reaching Today's Youth*.

Dr. Mendler has been recognized for his distinguished teaching in the areas of discipline, behavior, and classroom management by the Bureau of Education and Research, and he was a recipient of the coveted Crazy Horse Award for having made outstanding contributions to discouraged youth.

Dr. Mendler lives with his wife, Barbara, and his daughter, Lisa, in Rochester, NY.

For more information, please visit the Teacher Learning Center, LLC, Web site at www.TLC-SEMS.com.

Introduction

In a seminar for teachers, held in a small South Texas border town, we were discussing with participants the best ways to defuse angry and hostile students. Ms. Stevens, an eighth-grade math teacher, mentioned that just the other day she'd used humor to defuse a situation with a student in her class who is very troubled. I (Brian Mendler) wasn't sure what she meant until she told us about Miguel. Ms. Stevens warned the group that Miguel occasionally used inappropriate language, but none of us had any idea that it was as bad as it was. The boy was about six feet tall and could be quite intimidating. His black hair was halfway down his back. He wore boots with thick heels. His tank top displayed muscles normally seen on a man in his mid-twenties. His baseball cap was always on backwards and his dark brown eyes were piercing. Miguel was known as a fighter, often stirring up trouble with other kids. His home life was a mess. His father was in jail and his mother worked three jobs in order to support Miguel and his three younger brothers. They lived in a small trailer on the outskirts of town, with few legitimate employment opportunities but an energetic school staff.

"All the other students were already working on their assignment. All I did was ask him to take out his notebook and a pen," Ms. Stevens told the seminar. "He glared at me and in a deep and nasty tone replied, 'I ain't gonna do what you say you skinny ugly bitch.'"

Dead silence fell on Ms. Stevens's room as the students awaited her reply. "I was sick of the same old response,"

Ms. Stevens told the seminar participants. "I'd already written him up 58 times. I constantly removed him and this was where that had gotten us. He was no better. He still hated my class and me. He was still rude, disrespectful, and defiant. Miguel was succeeding in making my life miserable, but I decided that today would be different. I decided that just for today he was not going to get to me. I would not be defeated in my own classroom. I would not let him win. So with the sternest face I could muster I walked directly over to Miguel. I was standing about two feet from his chiseled frame. I looked right into his eyes and with all the energy I could muster, I replied, "You think I'm skinny? That's the best news I've heard all year! Finally someone thinks I'm skinny. Get over here, Miguel, so I can give you a hug. Hang on everyone; I need to call my husband! Miguel thinks I'm skinny!" A roar of laughter filled the seminar room.

"I hugged that boy as tight as I could," she told our group. "And then, right there in class, I called my husband. 'Honey, can you believe Miguel just called me skinny? He just got the entire class a night free of homework by complimenting me.'

"Way to go, Miguel," my husband bellowed back through the phone as I held it up to the class so they could hear that I really was talking to him." Ms. Stevens then looked at us and said, "For the first time all year, Miguel was speechless. He was defused. It looked as if his bubble had been burst. I smiled at him and, finally, he smiled back." "You got me, Ms. Stevens. That was a good one," Miguel said. "For the first time, Miguel and I connected. Without saying another word, he took out a pen and began taking notes." Ms. Stevens then added, "Isn't it amazing how our spouse or significant other knows our most difficult students better than anyone else in our class?"

So true, I thought. For me, the name wasn't Miguel, but I knew everyone in that room could relate to these challenges, which we all face daily.

What Ms. Stevens said to Miguel was truly remarkable and not easy to do. It required skill, determination, and courage. In fact, many of the things discussed in this book will not be easy to do. We are not interested in the easy way out if no progress is seen. We don't think it takes a whole lot of skill to write kids up and throw them out. Anyone can do that. Anyone can give a detention, or an extended detention, or an in-school suspension, or an out-of-school suspension. We want to be better. We want you to be better. We want to defuse and disarm hostile and explosive situations before they happen. We are interested in two things at all times: We want to keep students in class, and we want to get back to teaching. Those are our goals. That is what Ms. Stevens did, and boy, did she look tough in front of her class.

This book contains many anecdotes about our teaching experiences. For the sake of clarity, we will introduce each anecdote with the initials of the author who is telling the story.

We have shared stories like Ms. Stevens's numerous times at different workshops across the country. They usually inspire other teachers to tell their stories about challenging student behavior. In Tallahassee, Florida, a diminutive lady, Ms. Hall (who was 77 years young) raised her hand. "You're never going to believe what one of my students said to me just the other day. His name was Bill. He told me that he wasn't going take out his books, and then asked me how many times I had had sex with my husband. The whole class was watching. You could hear a pin drop. When I didn't answer immediately, he asked if I was ignoring him. I looked him square in the eye and said, 'No, I was just counting.' The whole class cracked up. Bill actually laughed too." He shook Ms. Hall's hand and knew that from then on he would have to try making some other teacher mad. Ms. Hall wasn't going to bite.

Our parents taught us that "sticks and stones will break our bones but names will never harm us." This sound advice can be extremely difficult to implement when our buttons are pushed. Yet, when these moments occur, real-life opportunities exist to teach our students how to handle hurtful behavior that may come their way. We must find ways of getting beyond, "You said *what* to me? No one uses that tone of voice with me. Get out and don't come back until you are ready to learn!"

Teaching students who are difficult and hostile takes effort and preparation. These kids are not easy. Since they mostly don't trust adults, they try their best to make our lives miserable. They believe we will quit on them just as everyone else has. When we don't, they often get temporarily worse, trying to prove to themselves that we will give up but secretly hoping we won't. It is difficult but possible to train ourselves to understand this dynamic. It is difficult but possible to learn not to be instinctive in our responses, but to think things through. It is difficult but possible to train our ear to hear what kids are saying instead of how they are saying it. It is difficult but possible to connect with difficult students and influence change. Working with students who are difficult is not easy, but it can be extremely rewarding and it is a part of the job. We are not paid to just teach the "good" students or the "smart" students or the "happy" students or the "normal" students. Great teachers teach the students they are given. They don't complain, they don't whine, and they don't waste time.

Like all decent people, Ms. Stevens and Ms. Hall were undoubtedly offended by their students' remarks, but they chose to handle things with competence and dignity. In doing so, they earned the respect of these students and reinforced themselves as dependable even in tough times. They were attacked, but did not attack back. By not attacking back they were less likely to have these things said to them again. Both students unloaded their ammunition. They fired the best rockets they had and did no damage. This is one of the most powerful ways that kids learn to stop firing and how others learn what to do when fired at. A major key in dealing with aggressive behavior is learning how to stay personally connected without taking offensive behavior personally and then responding effectively without attacking. It takes confidence and skills that all educators can learn to effectively defuse potentially explosive situations. Our lives then become so much easier when working with students with behavior difficulties, and our schools become safer.

During the last decade or so, many schools have enacted zero tolerance policies in efforts to make schools safer. The result has been neither an increase in safety (schools always have been and remain among the safest places for kids) nor changed behavior among those who are excluded from school. Our belief is that we must embrace all students, particularly those who are the most challenging. More than anyone else, it is they who need better ways to cope, and we need them to discover more productive ways of redirecting and expressing their frustrations.

Do you ever wonder why some teachers have few, if any, behavior problems in their class? Why it is that Student A completely behaves in music class, but terrorizes the teacher in art class? What does the music teacher do that the art teacher doesn't? Why is it that certain teachers are the ones sought for the placement of tough kids? What do they do, how do they act and react? This book shares effective practices and offers practical, real-life suggestions, examples, and solutions to these problems from the perspective of the best classroom educators.

1

The Problem of Harmful Aggression

Harmful aggression, disruption, and even violence are all too common in our schools and classrooms. Unfortunately, they are a part of U.S. society. In the United States in 2002, firearms were the second-leading cause of death for children between the ages of 10 and 19, behind only motor vehicle accidents. In fact, during that same year firearms killed 71 preschool children, while 56 law-enforcement officers were killed in the line of duty (Children's Defense Fund, 2005). It is extraordinary that more preschoolers were killed than on-duty police officers. As we write this book, we mourn the victims of three horrific school shootings in less than a two-week period, the most shocking of which was in an Amish school where six young girls were shot to death and six more were wounded. While we understand that this incident was not the result of student-on-student violence, we are still deeply saddened and unnerved by this tragic event. The Virginia Tech massacre was another in a long line of tragedies related to kids, guns, and killing.

Many children with disruptive behavior come from troubled homes. These students are frequently on the move, jumping from relative to relative with no stable home. With movement comes change, and many of our disruptive youth have experienced much change. According to Walls (2003), more than 500,000 third graders had already attended more than three schools between first and third grade. It takes four to six months for each student to recover academically from a transfer. These students are half as likely to graduate from high school as kids who do not move between schools, and their attendance rates are much lower than the national average (Walls, 2003).

The causes of unbridled harmful aggression are complex and often interwoven. Abused children often grow up to be abusive adults who perpetuate a cycle of violence directed toward those they can victimize—and each year, two to three million children are reportedly abused in this country. Other causes of aggression include the continuing erosion of the nurturing family structure, the absence of fathers in the home, increasing depersonalization within communities, drug use, turf wars caused by drugs and the profit motive, and a diminishing impact of community values. In one class I (BDM) taught last year, three of my five unmarried male students were to be fathers within the year.

For those who are not within a nurturing and healthy family, gangs become a substitute family. Others join gangs out of fear or for the excitement they envision. Society used to bemoan gang members who "rumbled" with switchblades. Now, with incredibly easy access to handguns and combat weapons, shootings and their far more destructive effects are common.

Too often, the media glorify harmful aggression as a natural way of life, barraging impressionable youth with images of death and violence. According to Herr (2005), parents spend an average of three and a half minutes a week in meaningful conversation with each of their children. These same children average more than 1,600 minutes (almost 27 hours) in front of the television set, often with violent images streaking across the screen. Even more startling is that the average child will have witnessed close to 8,000 murders on television by the end of elementary school (Herr, 2005). With so little guidance from parents, it is not surprising that many youth carry the aggression, hostility, and violence they see on television into the classroom with them. According to Larsen (2003), there are some factors that increase the likelihood of violence in school: When the male population increases, so does aggression. The larger the student population, the greater the prevalence of violence and aggression in schools.

RLC had an in-depth discussion with Brooks Brown. Brown was a best friend of Eric Harris, who was one of the shooters at Columbine High School, Colorado, in 2000 (the other shooter was Dylan Klebold). He talked about how he and his friends played videogames that encouraged shooting people and how they loved the killing part. "Killing was so much fun," he said. Reportedly, Harris and Klebold watched the movie *Natural Born Killers* a few hundred times. We cannot say whether the games or movie influenced Harris or Klebold. We *can* say with some certainty that the relationship between kids and the media is not always healthy.

Messages of humility are hard to come by. Commercials often promote the acquisition of quick and easy goods and status. Music videos saturate youth with images of violence, beautiful women, diamonds, expensive clothes, and pricey sneakers. Television shows have capitalized on the fantasies of teenagers as well. Extreme makeovers where men and women become "new" people are becoming increasingly popular. Of course, rarely do the networks show the person working hard to attain a "great body." Usually we get to see the surgery that cuts away the fat. Why work hard over a long period of time in the gym and go through the discomfort of changing your diet when you can just go under the knife and get the same new look? We can turn on the television at any time of the day or night and find someone winning huge money at the poker table. Unfortunately, the game of choice in study hall and the cafeteria is now "Texas Hold 'Em." Instead of kids pretending to be the next Michael Jordan, they want to be the next Chris "Jesus" Ferguson. Instant gratification is in!

What's next? A reality show in a bar showing how many beers a person can shotgun without throwing up? How about a chain-smoking reality show? Let's see how many cigarettes you can smoke without choking.

On a global level, hatred based on religious, cultural, or sexual differences is on the rise. When tens of thousands riot and burn buildings because of an unflattering cartoon depicting the prophet Mohammed, and suicide bombing carried out against innocent civilians becomes an acceptable form of warfare approved by too many religious leaders, is it any wonder that violence is viewed as an acceptable way to solve problems? We cannot solve all of the world's problems, but schools have an imperative to teach better ways of handling aggression, in less harmful and even productive ways. Although it is easy to grow sick and tired of trying to understand the causes of unbridled harmful aggression, it is important that we understand what affects our students' behavior so that we can more effectively deal with its effects in our classrooms.

AGGRESSION AND SOCIETY

Aggression is part of our makeup. It is human nature to occasionally be aggressive toward someone. We need to teach students that there are times and places where aggression is acceptable. We need to point aggressive youngsters in the direction of the football field, wrestling mat, or even the boxing ring or octagon. These kids need to learn how to channel the aggression to the places where it is appropriate and even useful.

I (BDM) was recently playing golf in Florida with two 25-year veterans of the Miami-Dade Police Department. They shared stories of drug busts, gang fights, and unruly drunks. After a few minutes, they asked me what I did for a living. When I told them I was a high school teacher working in a tough district outside of Rochester with emotionally challenging 16- and 17-year-old kids they both looked at me with bewilderment. One told me I was crazy, and with a completely straight face said, "That job is way too dangerous for me. I have no idea how you do it." Thinking about that exchange later, I wondered where our society had gone. Did these two hulking police officers really think that working in a school with kids was more dangerous than the police beat in Miami? Unfortunately, it seemed they did. Both appeared to breathe a sigh of relief that they were able to return to their nice, cushy jobs of patrolling the streets and arresting thieves and murderers in southern Florida.

During our discussion, one of the officers asked why so much of the literature his young son brought home dealt with violence and aggression. It occurred to me later that much of the curriculum has aggression and violence associated with it. While Shakespeare is one of the most marvelous writers of all time, and the lessons that can be learned from his work are many, his plays are often tragic and brutally violent. In many schools, the ninth-grade curriculum includes his classic *Macbeth*, a story where greed, deception, and lies lead to murder. Shakespeare is not the only author who deals in death, of course. It is not Shakespeare or any other author that creates a problem. Rather, the problem is that violence is accepted by our culture as a natural way of life.

Despite the many positive moral lessons in John Steinbeck's *Of Mice and Men*, George shoots his best friend Lennie in the back of the head. Mention S. E. Hinton's *The Outsiders* to a high school student and you will hear what a great book it is. Of course, the main premise is that Socias and Greasers battle for supremacy, and the climax of the book is an all-out rumble between the two gangs. Again, violence is at the core an American classic. *West Side Story*, a modern retelling of Shakespeare's *Romeo and Juliet*, remains a popular musical performed by high school drama classes.

We do not mean to imply that literature, plays, or schools are the cause of aggression and violence. In fact, we believe that one of the best ways to get students to pay attention in class and not disrupt others is to teach curriculum based on what students relate to. That said, it is important to understand that aggression continues to be as much a reality in schools as in society, despite the fact that school remains the safest sanctuary for many children who are confronted with daily assaults to their physical and psychological well-being.

We can make a difference

The problem with a lot of school interventions is that they do not get to the root of the problem. Too often, simplistic solutions such as "just say no" or "zero tolerance" become the blueprints for our "solutions."

Author Brian Mendler recently consulted in a school outside Dallas, Texas, and has this to say about the experience: As I pulled up to the school, I could not help but notice the gorgeous athletic facilities. The football stadium sat 15,000, the baseball diamond's pristine grass was perfectly manicured, and the track was brand new. Each facility had a set of powerful lights for evening games and events. Then I walked inside the dark, dreary school. The auditorium was old and run down. In fact, the principal had a hard time finding a microphone that worked. I told him it seemed a bit ironic that the athletic facilities were better than most colleges I had seen, but microphones for conference days were scarce. He told me that the fields were so beautiful because taxpayers will approve spending money only when it includes renovating an athletic facility. He told me that the school did its best to "sneak textbooks and other essential items" into those proposals.

Although nice athletic complexes are hardly the root of unacceptable aggression, how we prioritize is part of the problem. As much as we would like to, we cannot fix the home lives of our children, change how many television shows they watch or video games they play, or even change how our school board develops its priorities. Our goal must be to maximize the time we have with them at school to improve the quality of their lives. We must make schools and classrooms inviting, relevant places where students want to be. We must work as hard as we can to make our schools and classrooms more appealing than the local mall or arcade, and more attractive to them than playing their favorite video game. Great teachers can take a show like *MTV Cribs* and teach an economics or math lesson directly from the conversation students are having about it. Lessons on probability can connect to their fascination with poker. Most important, while we have them, there is much we can do to teach that hurting others is wrong, that there are nonaggressive ways to get what they want, and that success in school and ultimately in life is absolutely possible.

What is harmful aggression?

Harmful aggression is an assault on a person that can take three forms: body (physical injury), esteem (verbal harassment such as name calling toward the teacher or another student), or property (damage to things one owns). Often, harmful aggression is bred in an atmosphere of hostility where it feels and looks better to hurt than to resolve and tolerate. All educators realize that learning is seriously affected when children and teachers feel unsafe. Learning cannot flourish when students are worried about being hurt, put down, or having things they value defaced or destroyed.

Discover and define new possibilities

Read the following exchange between Bill, a graduate student, and his professor after a tough day at his teaching job:

Bill: I cannot get these kids to stop talking. They just will not shut up. What do you do with kids who are constantly talking?

Professor: What are they talking about?

Bill: I have no idea, and who cares anyway. They should be listening to me.

Professor: Okay, what are you trying to teach them?

Bill: Vocabulary. I'm a French teacher and these kids have to learn the vocabulary.

Professor: Are you sure you don't know what they were talking about?

Bill: (*getting more disgusted*) I guess they were yapping about the Yankees game last night. You know kids; all they talk about are sports, music, and video games.

Professor: What vocabulary words were you trying to teach?

Bill: Colors and numbers.

We couldn't help but wonder what would happen if Bill engaged his students about the game and said something like, "You know guys, I hear you talking about the game last night. How do you say the word 'Yankees' in French? What is the French word for the color of their uniforms? By the way, what was the score? Who can say it in French?"

We sometimes get so caught up in trying to teach the curriculum that we miss opportunities to capture the energy of our students by blending their interests with what we are expected to teach. If we are always concerned with stopping a behavior, we might miss a great opportunity to teach our content by using what students do or say as a bridge to the lesson. We will discuss this important concept in Chapter 5, Classroom Strategies for the Teacher.

THIS BOOK

Strategies for Successful Classroom Management describes practical methods of prevention: things educators can do to minimize the likelihood that students will act in aggressive and disruptive ways at school. This volume provides many methods of action: ways of behaving and communicating with students when they are engaging in challenging and potentially explosive behaviors. This volume also describes skills that students can learn to make them better at identifying "anger triggers" so they can choose alternatives to violent responses. This approach, first described in the book *Discipline With Dignity* (Curwin & Mendler, 1988, 1999), continues to be very effective in helping thousands of educators establish best practices in their classrooms.

This book was written with the lofty goal and fervent hope that children can be taught to internalize nonviolent and nonaggressive ways to handle their emotions. The curriculum of the twenty-first century must include skills in how to get along with each other, which is as close to the basics as a society can ever hope to get. Without these skills and knowledge, no other learning will matter much. Effective programs can change the way children think and behave. Schools can and should lead the way to a safer and saner future.

This book is a prayer and a response to the problem of aggression and disruption. Solving this problem requires a long-term commitment: a commitment to the belief that all children have value and that every act of aggression and violence against them is a crime against our way of life, our most cherished values, and our belief in the future of all our students.

2

Attitudes, Beliefs, and Principles for Educators

The following beliefs and principles underlie strategies for effectively preventing harmful and disruptive behavior, as well as handling problems effectively when they occur.

TEACHING STUDENT BEHAVIOR: PART OF THE JOB

Many educators are frustrated with the growing demands placed on them to be all things to all students, so it is understandable that demands for teaching social skills, peacemaking, and conflict mediation are met with skepticism and diffidence. However, if we truly want to be successful with all students and our response to disruption is to remove a student, we should not be surprised when that same child comes back the next day behaving exactly the same way. We need to teach better behavior every day if we are going to motivate students to change.

Liz was a very bright girl who craved constant attention. We worked together on a daily basis, and I (BDM) began to form a bond with her, or so I thought. On a cold Monday in January, Liz came in and for no reason that I could discern punched me in the arm. I looked at her and asked why she had hit me. Liz responded by laughing and punching me again. She hit me a few more times that day. After work I told her social worker what had happened. He explained that the only form of affection Liz ever saw were her parents hitting each other. They would first yell, then punch and kick each other. The social worker explained that those behaviors were actually signs of affection, and said he would not be surprised if the aggression increased until she learned a nonviolent way to show she cared.

Those of us who have been nurtured in loving families have a hard time understanding Liz's behavior. Armed with the background of her behavior, though, I was able to avoid getting mad and disciplining Liz. Instead, I made it a goal to help her learn other, more appropriate ways of showing affection and to spend a few minutes every day just being a caring person in her life.

Teach the behavior you want to see

Sometimes students do not know how to behave. It is not unusual to see students sitting in a detention room for a pre-determined amount of time without anyone instructing them on what they have done wrong and how to correct their behavior. It is no wonder that most of these students come back to class the following day and behave exactly the same way. Think about something in your life outside of school that you do well. Now think about the first or second time that you ever tried this. Were you good at it immediately? Did you know how to drive a car the first time you ever got behind the wheel? Or the first time you ever cooked, played a sport, sang a song, or danced? Were you good right away?

A few might have been masters immediately, but if you are like most people, it took time to acquire your skill. Think about how you improved. What did you do to make yourself stronger in that area? Again, if you are like most people, you improved because you practiced.

Most students do not get real opportunities to practice improving their behavior. More common is for them to be punished by denying them opportunities to practice. How can a student demonstrate good behavior on the playground if recess time is spent inside with the teachers? Is it reasonable for us to expect students to learn better behavior on field trips if their punishment is missing a field trip? A better strategy is to say something like, "Until you show me you can behave yourself on the playground, I guess I'll have to stay out there with you to make sure you remember to use your words rather than your fists when you are angry. I'm sure it won't take you long to remember, though. I am confident that by the end of the week you will be able to be out there without me watching your every move." Responding in this way may take more work initially, but has a far better chance of leading to better behavior in the long term.

We hope that pointing out the obvious is not necessary. Of course, if a kid is throwing rocks on the playground, do something! Just don't expect the student to improve at being on the playground while inside with you.

You can't always treat everyone in exactly the same way

Most classrooms have several, or even many, students. This means different minds, thoughts, feelings, and home lives. Is it realistic to treat each one of them in exactly the same way? Being effective means that we do whatever is necessary with each student to promote success and responsibility. Since many of us were trained to believe that good discipline requires a consistent approach, many schools persist in offering the same consequences and procedures to all students, regardless of their individual circumstance or developmental appropriateness. For example, some schools with a zero tolerance policy on student aggression have felt compelled to call the police about a kindergarten student biting the teacher.

Another school recently dealt with a female teacher who was bald from chemotherapy treatment by requiring her to remove a bandana she wore because of the school's "no hats in school" rule. To their credit, the entire science department at the school wore bandanas in sympathy the next day and the school backed down. Being fair means giving people what they need; equal means treating everyone the same. Be fair; do not worry about treating everyone the same. In Chapter 4, we present strategies to teach your students so that you will never hear the words "that's not fair" again.

Strategies and interventions work best when based primarily on values, rather than on rewards and punishments. This volume advocates creating clear rules that are predicated on a set of values taught to students. When rule violations occur, educators need a range of available consequences that they can implement to teach the students more responsible behavior. When danger or safety is an issue, obedience-based discipline methods are important. However, the main focus in reducing harmful aggression is assisting students to develop a sense of responsibility. Obedience-based discipline relies heavily on threats, rewards, and punishments. The goal becomes identifying either adequate rewards or sufficiently noxious punishments. Because there is a heavy reliance on the use of external methods of control, authorities must always be visible to enforce policy. Rewards and punishments can be useful for short-term benefit, but long-term change is fueled by methods that teach and reinforce proper values such as safety, altruism, caring, respect—and, most important, remorse.

Only strong values motivate us to control our naturally aggressive nature. Before a nonviolent choice can be made, an individual needs a potent desire to make that choice. Students must believe in their minds, hearts, and spirits that hurting others is wrong.

Behavior change among hardened, antisocial, and angry students will not occur simply because a teacher offers more love, caring, and decision-making opportunities (which are all necessary components in developing responsibility).

Conventional behavioral methods that are obedience oriented ("Do as I say and you will be rewarded, or punished if you do not") are occasionally useful in the early stages for such youth and for those around them to feel a sense of safety and security. But since school is primarily a place of education, its primary focus is creating responsible decision making among youth who lack either the skill or the will to do what is right.

A school district outside Chicago recently, in 2005, encouraged its students to be involved in reducing violence. The children filled their halls with antiviolence posters, put on an assembly about violence prevention, and invented a slogan to say when tensions mounted: "It's okay to walk away." The school, which prefers to remain anonymous, reported a significant decrease in violent behaviors that year.

As educators, we do not simply wish to teach children to rise above their impulses, drives, and emotions. We want to teach them to reach out and aspire to a higher dimension, one inhabited by values, a strong sense of what is right as well as what is wrong, and an understanding and belief in the essential sanctity of the human spirit.

The only person you can control is yourself, so stay in control of yourself

It is easy to get as worked up as the students we teach. Often, the louder and more animated they get, the louder and more animated *we* get. That behavior on our part rarely solves the problem of control. In fact, the opposite works best. Teachers and administrators need to remain as calm as possible, *especially* during moments of disruption and chaos.

When we travel the country visiting and consulting in schools, we are sometimes shocked at how some define "classroom control." Recently, a principal proudly confided that one of her best teachers never had behavior problems because the kids were "terrified to utter a peep." Just take a moment right now to think about what you would say if someone asked you the meaning of classroom control?

If your answer begins like many educators, you are think-ing "the kids are quiet, the kids are listening, the kids are learn-ing, the kids are paying attention, the kids are not speaking, the kids are raising their hands, the kids, the kids, the kids . . ." Actually, though, *classroom control* means that we are in control of the only person we have control over—ourselves. Students behave best when they are around a confident teacher who is not easily rattled by the ups and downs of life.

Great athletes are fantastic at controlling themselves. They thrive on the road, where the crowd is hostile, the stadium is loud, and the referees don't give them the calls. Michael Jordan never blamed the fans after missing a crucial shot. Tiger Woods does not blame the gallery when he misses a putt. Great athletes do not get flustered with even the most vulgar of fans. Instead, they ask for the ball. They thrive on the pressure. And over an entire season or a long tournament, they come out on top. Great athletes spend a great deal of time preparing for the crucial moment so they can step back when chaos surrounds them, survey the situation, and execute a winning game plan. The greatest quarterbacks in football all share the quality of being calm under pressure.

We encourage you to emulate these stars. Establish an effec-tive classroom by building strong, positive relationships. We ask you to make learning relevant and set kids up for success. Really engage them by listening to them, and by promoting an atmosphere of fun. In addition, identify basic procedures such as how to enter the classroom, hand in papers, and what to do if you're late. Preparation before problems occur helps keep us calm during the chaotic moments so that we can step back to assess the situation and execute a winning strategy.

It is important to model this approach for our students. If we, the teachers and administrators, get as upset or angry as the students, we show that we are willing to lower ourselves to that emotional level. In fact, students learn that they cannot count on us when things get tough. They learn that we will fold under pressure and give in to our difficult surroundings. If our response to their misbehavior is to yell, we should not be surprised when they yell back. If our response is zero tolerance or throwing kids out of the classroom, we should not be surprised when they have zero tolerance for each other and dismiss each other just as abruptly.

Optimism is crucial, so you need to take good emotional care of yourself

Too few noneducation professionals truly appreciate the incredible outflow of energy, dedication, and commitment required to make a difference in the lives of students who come from troubled, dysfunctional environments. To keep from burning yourself out and to sustain your optimistic attitude, take good emotional care of yourself. Great coaches often exhort their athletes to "get your heads in the game." It is impossible to be successful teaching students with behavior difficulties without believing that the kids we are working with can and will be successful. In other words, our heads always have to be in the game. Every morning when the alarm clock rings we have to get out of bed, put our feet on the floor, look in the mirror and decide that today will be the day that little Johnny finally turns around his challenging behavior.

It can be difficult to want your disruptive, uncooperative, noncompliant students to show up. Have you noticed that they always are the kids that win the perfect attendance award? We are in class for the first 20 minutes, cruising along, beginning to hit our stride, when all of a sudden Johnny comes strutting in, knocking into desks, banging tables, and doing any other annoying thing he can to try to get our attention. To say the least, it can be really difficult to want to greet him with, "Good morning! Nice to see you today." Yet, like it or not, Johnny is a part of the class and we are required to teach him. And teaching him becomes a much better possibility when he knows he is wanted.

We often hear colleagues say things like, "That student doesn't belong in my class. There is no way that student can be successful here. That student should be in an 'alternative school.'" Although ours may not be the ideal environment for all students, we must believe in their capacity for success, do our best to help the students to achieve success, and persist in trying to reach each of them. Without this attitude, there truly is no hope of facilitating change.

Students with difficult, disruptive, or dangerous behaviors can easily evoke fear and anger in their teachers. Recognize these feelings, and create a system of support for yourself. Take a short walk during lunch or preparation time during school. Talk to a trusted colleague about what you feel, or talk to a colleague about a subject other than school. Take a "sick-of-kids" day once or twice a year and do something fun for yourself. This use of sick leave is just as legitimate as taking a sick day when you have the flu. Do all that you can to stay physically and emotionally healthy. You will be a more effective and helpful teacher if you feel fit in every way.

Stay personally connected to students without taking personally what they say or do

Emotionally scarred and wounded students have learned to hate. Because important others have treated them with abuse or have been unable to nurture them, these students view the world as hostile. Expecting hostility, they act first and do provocative things to make others angry. Provoked adults often become angry at the student and say or do something to show they're boss. Having made yet another adult feel hostile, the student's worldview is confirmed. This "hostility cycle" continues uninterrupted until adults who regularly participate in the life of the hostile student understand this dynamic and refuse to play the game.

When a student like Frank votes on a class assignment by raising his middle finger, we must fight the impulse to say, "I'm sick of it, Frank. Get out and don't come back until you are ready to stop insulting me." It is instead okay to say, in a calm voice, "Frank, I can see that you are opposed to the assignment I'm giving. We both know there are better ways to voice your vote." Later on, in private, firmly let him know that his behavior was unacceptable and that you will not tolerate behaviors that seek to embarrass you in front of the class. Perhaps at that time you might wish to give a consequence. Most important is to be sure that he knows a more acceptable way to express himself in the future. Also, make a point of reaching out to him in a positive way soon thereafter.

Great teachers are able to continue teaching their lessons without getting sidetracked with discipline problems. Students with behavior difficulties test us to see if they can distract us. Great teachers show early on that they will not always stop their lesson. In fact, many will pick up on what a tough student says, and teach a lesson based on it.

I (BDM) am reminded of a student I had in an "emotionally disturbed" special education class. There were about 15 kids and it was not uncommon for someone to walk in dropping "F-Bombs" or saying something inappropriate. On this day, Jenna walked in and bellowed, "Yo, Mr. M, Alex Rodriguez [the baseball player] is f***ing hot."

At this moment I had a choice. I could address the inappropriate language, or I could continue teaching. I responded by saying, "And I'm about to show you 250 million reasons he is even hotter than you think. He signed a 10-year, $250 million contract to play baseball." I then asked Jenna to come up front and write the number 250,000,000 on the board. After a few incorrect attempts she got the proper amount of zeros, to which I responded, "Great job, Jenna. By the way, how much money does he make per year?" After some quick division, she looked at me and said "$25 million"?

"Yup, very good, but we really need to know how much money he makes for each game. So Jenna, there are 162 games in a season. How do we figure out how much he makes per game?" Ben chimed in, "Just divide $25 million by 162. And I already did it, Mr. M. It is about $154,000 per game." Jenna was visibly happy. Ben then said, "And guess how much he makes per inning?" He answered his own question, "About $17,000." To which Jenna gleefully exclaimed, "So Mr. Mendler, he only has to play three innings of one game, and he makes more than you do for an entire year. And he doesn't even have to work with us!"

This unplanned lesson lasted about 20 minutes. I then looked at the class and said, "Okay guys, enough talk about Alex Rodriguez. Now we need to do some math." Of course, I was already teaching math, probably better than I had all year long. They were engaged, listening, learning, and participating. It all happened because I didn't take the bait that Jenna dangled and become angry, start lecturing about proper language, or write up a referral. After class I had a private conversation with Jenna about a more appropriate way to express her feelings about Alex Rodriguez.

Model the skills you want students to use

Students sometimes use harmful aggression as a way of satisfying one or more of their basic needs. They may be expressing anger or frustration, showing off, seeking a sense of control, or protecting themselves. Conflict resolution, peer mediation, and anger control are examples of existing programs that teach students nonviolent ways to settle disputes and meet their needs.

All school personnel—teachers, administrators, custodians, counselors, lunchroom monitors, and school bus drivers—need to model the choices and behaviors when they are angry that they want their students to use. No student can do what he or she has never seen. By modeling the skills we want students to use when they are faced with difficult moments, we show that real people use nonviolent strategies and that these can work even when people are upset.

It is best to respond in the same manner expected of the angry student: "I'd prefer you didn't raise your voice and yell at me. However, I can see why you might be upset about it. Let's chat about this later and come up with a solution. Thanks for sharing, and remember I welcome your enthusiasm." If we are truly seeking to teach students how to handle frustration in a productive way, modeling how to do it is the only real way of gaining their trust.

Teach students how to make effective choices

We learn to be responsible by making choices and experiencing the positive or negative results of the choices we make. When students break rules or behave disruptively, they need both firm limits and real choices. Firm limits show that we mean business about what will or will not be accepted. Real choices help students realize that they are capable of selecting better alternatives. We should express firm limits and the reasons for those limits. The limits should surround the choices we are giving. For example, "Jamil, it is unacceptable to not do any of the homework problems [limit] because you won't get any practice and I won't know how you are doing [reason for the limit]. I can live with you choosing any five problems that will best show both of us that you understand the material [choice]. However, it is unacceptable to do none [limit]. Thanks." Think of choices as the meat of a good sandwich. The limits and the reasons for the limits are the bread: LIMIT (Reason for the limit) ... CHOICE ... CHOICE ... CHOICE ... LIMIT (Reason for the limit).

Students often behave better and learn the value of responsibility when they have a say in what happens to them. People are more likely to follow rules that they helped create, and that make sense to them. It is much easier to correct an inappropriate behavior when an offending student had a say in making the rule that is broken. Students can be encouraged to propose rules and consequences at both classroom and schoolwide levels. One model is to have two student representatives from each grade level who make input regularly to a schoolwide committee about issues related to school rules and policies. We will discuss this further in Chapter 6.

Be willing to work with students we want to throw out or write up

Students almost always return to the classroom after an incident. When they do, it is important to welcome them back. We need to share our preference for things to never get as bad again as they were, and then teach them how to handle things more appropriately in the future. Doing this gives us an opportunity to model, to teach, and finally to have students practice alternative expressions of anger, frustration, and impatience.

As consultants, we are often asked by administrators how to get teachers to stop giving detentions. We suggest that teachers stay with the students they detain to explore possible solutions shortly after the incident. Good teachers are willing to "own" the consequence they give. Such a policy also puts an obstacle in the way of teachers who are quick to refer but unwilling to engage. Most teachers who have done this report better results because they are able to deal with the issues in a concentrated manner without other students looking on. When there is a chronic problem involving a teacher and student, administrators can show their teachers how to handle the interaction so that both the teacher and the student are pleased with the outcome.

Create and nurture community networks

With an emphasis on achieving standards of excellence for all students, coupled with the growth of inclusion, the diversity of learning needs is greater than ever. No matter how talented, a single teacher cannot simultaneously teach five reading groups, manage four students with attention deficit hyperactivity disorder, facilitate conflict mediation between two upset children, and take an autistic child for a walk. In recognition of this diversity, educators—particularly classroom teachers—must create a network of resources to meet students' needs. Parents, senior citizens, and volunteers can be called on to help make a difference in students' lives. Individual volunteers, as well as civic-minded community and business organizations, need to be recruited.

In 2005, the Bill and Melinda Gates Foundation (Bill Gates is the founder of Microsoft) donated $9.5 million to the Oakland, California, school district. At that time, Oakland schools graduated an average of 30 percent of their students, compared with a national average of 68 percent. The Urban Institute pegged Oakland's 52 percent as one of the highest dropout rates in the country (Asimov, 2005). The Gates

Foundation donation will go toward building more schools to reduce class sizes. Also, a portion of the money will be used to fund existing programs that were on the chopping block.

Businesses are making smaller-scale donations, too. In 2004, the GE Foundation established a scholarship in honor of retired broadcast icon Tom Brokaw. Each year, the company will give cash grants of $15,000 to two deserving high school seniors. The winners will get that amount of money each year for up to four years of college. GE will also give scholarships to seniors who have demonstrated a high level of community service involvement.

The reality is that every little bit helps. We encourage you to work with your school to seek relationships with local businesses, and to invite them to help make your school a better place. Many businesses are looking for positive publicity. Donating to schools is an easy way for businesses to look good in the public eye.

Always treat students with dignity

Successful educators convey a basic sense of respect to their students by listening, being open to feedback from them, explaining why they want things done a certain way, and giving students some choices in classroom affairs that affect them. They are able to respectfully insist on decent behavior because they are unafraid of calling attention to unacceptable words or actions without put-downs, sarcasm, scolds, and threats. The message they send is, "You are important, and so am I!"

It is difficult to feel dignified when students tell you where to go and how quickly they want you to get there. It is especially difficult when students challenge our professionalism. We can easily become cynical in such a climate, yet nothing exacerbates aggression and hostility faster than a cynical attitude. We must continually resist viewing and responding to troubling students as "worthless ingrates" and we must help less-experienced colleagues who are filled with vigor and enthusiasm by banning the "you'll see" faculty room chatter. Reacting with dignity to the very moments in which students are rendering indignities to each other and us sends a powerful message that shows capability and strength without resorting to brutality.

KEY POINTS FROM THE CHAPTER

It's important for educators to remember that sometimes students need to learn the behaviors we want to see. When we model these behaviors, our students are much more likely to adopt them. For example, when discussing an altercation with a student, Mr. Bilsky started the conversation like this:

Mr. Bilsky: Hi Tom. I just want to tell you that I'm sorry for embarrassing you in front of your friends. I should have found a better time and place to let you know that I wasn't pleased with your behavior. I will try hard not to do it again. So now that I've told you how I was wrong, is there anything you think you could have done differently?

By beginning the conversation with what he did wrong, Mr. Bilsky modeled the behavior he wanted to see. Tom was then much more likely to admit his role in the incident.

One of the hardest things a teacher can do is remain optimistic with difficult and disruptive students. We must believe in the success of every single student put in front of us if we are to be successful with them. This is much easier when we are able to stay personally connected to each student without taking personally what they say or do.

A few other things to remember:

- Always treat students with dignity and respect (even if they don't reciprocate).
- Create, nurture, and sustain community relationships. Many are financially willing to help and make themselves look good in the process.
- Be sure to offer effective real-life choices and then allow students to live with the consequences of those choices.
- Use your instincts. Great teachers have a plan but allow themselves to deviate from that plan if necessary.

3

Why Kids Misbehave and What to Do About It

E ducators are more effective when they take time to understand the underlying reasons behind why kids misbehave. If we don't understand why, treating the misbehavior is
much more difficult. If two people have a headache, one might
have minor eye strain and another might have a brain tumor.
Naturally, the treatment for each would be drastically differently, even though the symptom is exactly the same.

It is often difficult to figure out why a kid is misbehaving.
To simplify, virtually every student who misbehaves fits into
one of the following four categories: they lack awareness, they
believe they are stupid or hopeless, they want to look good in
front of their friends, or they are seeking attention.

STUDENTS WHO LACK AWARENESS

Sometimes students are just unaware of what they are doing. Do
you have the dreaded pencil tapper in your class? Sometimes
pencil and pen tappers are tapping to annoy us. Other times,

though, they are engrossed in deep thought and are not aware of their behavior. The way to know the difference is usually when asking the unaware student to stop, they do. They will usually resume soon after, without being aware that they are doing so.

Jen Swenk, a fifth-grade teacher, told us that she keeps a small scrap of carpeting taped to each desk. She asks her students to please tap on the carpet if they need to do so. She realized that it wasn't the actual tapping but the noise from the tapping that caused her to become annoyed. By eliminating the noise, she also eliminated the disruption.

Students with awareness issues are generally disorganized and forgetful. They are often very nice kids, but seem aloof and lost. They make excuses—"I had no idea the homework was due today"—and usually are telling the truth.

When the teacher lacks awareness, problem behavior can be triggered. I (BDM) am reminded of a time my little "brother," Victor, got in trouble. I have been a volunteer in the Big Brothers Big Sisters program for the past five years. Victor, my little "brother," is currently in seventh grade at a tough inner-city public school. I recently received a call from his grandmother, Barbara. She told me that his teacher had called to report that Victor was being "insubordinate." She told me that he refused to take his sweatshirt off in school. She said that the school had a rule prohibiting students from wearing anything that could be conceived as gang related. Barbara explained that the rule actually had to do with hoods: students were not permitted to wear anything with a hood. Unknown to me, Victor told the teacher that he was wearing a four-year-old t-shirt with holes that was too short under the sweatshirt. He was unaware of the "no-hood" rule and promised not to wear it again if he could just keep it on that day. He didn't want to be embarrassed the rest of the day, but the teacher refused to comply. As the argument ensued, Victor raised his voice to the teacher, exclaiming that there was no way he was taking the f***ing sweatshirt off. The teacher did not tolerate that offensive language. Barbara was called. Victor got a two-day suspension.

Although this type of language is inappropriate and should not be tolerated in school, what should have been a minor exchange between a teacher and a student turned into an argument and a suspension, and left neither person feeling good about the interaction. While the teacher was doing her best to follow the rules of the school, sometimes we need to back off for the good of the individual. Victor was not going to take the sweatshirt off, and the teacher should have realized that in the first few minutes of the exchange. With this in mind, it would have been a good thing for the teacher to remind the entire class that it is "not okay to wear hoods in class or in school. However, Victor has a special circumstance today. This will be the last time I see him or anyone else wear sweatshirts with hoods. Thanks for understanding." This was a potentially explosive situation that could have been de-escalated by a skilled teacher.

By approaching it this way, the teacher maintains control of the class, addresses the problem, and reiterates her position that it is inappropriate to wear a hood in class. The teacher also shows her students that she is capable of understanding different situations that come up, and is willing to address them on an individual basis (see Chapter 4, Fair Versus Equal).

Many special education students disrupt class because of awareness issues. I (RLC) am reminded of Alex, a fourth grader classified as learning disabled (LD). Reading was his problem. Alex struggled because he kept confusing the letters *p, d, q,* and *b,* which made reading a terribly painful process for him. Some teachers would say about him, "If he paid attention to himself as much as he paid attention to others, he would be fine." Alex suffered from a problem that plagues many LD students: they constantly point out everyone else's mistakes. This happens because when you take a bright person who is constantly failing, they become hypersensitive to the failure of others so they don't feel so alone (Lavoie, 1989).

As Richard Lavoie so brilliantly points out in his video *The F.A.T. City Workshop* (1989), the problem was that Alex believed spatial orientation (the direction we view an object) did not determine object identification (what that object was). For example, look at the shirt you are wearing right now. Think about turning it around. Would it still be a shirt? Now imagine folding it. Is it still a shirt? What if you flipped it inside out? Is it still a shirt? Of course, it is a shirt no matter what direction you view it from. A student with a reading disability often stumbles over letters that appear alike because the brain is seeing the straight line and round circle attached to it and thinks it is always the same letter. A solution for Alex was to use books on tape. He followed along as he listened to a reader decode the different letters. The more Alex saw and heard the letters (repetition), the better he got at seeing the difference. In his case, the disruptive behavior he exhibited was really an awareness issue.

STUDENTS WHO BELIEVE THEY ARE STUPID OR SURE TO FAIL

Three weeks into a new school year my principal informed me (BDM) that I would be "blending" with a regular education teacher in a beginning Spanish class that was "out of control." I have never taken Spanish and the word *hola* was about the extent of my speaking ability. I was told that it didn't matter if I could speak Spanish. The teacher needed help managing behavior. If I could help with that, she would teach the Spanish. Fair enough, I thought.

Linda Williams was a 33-year-old teacher with 11 years of experience who immediately informed me that this was the worst class she had ever had in her teaching career. There were 23 students, 11 of them in beginning Spanish for the second time. Problems began with approximately 10 students arriving late daily and disrupting what she was doing. She was tired of writing referrals, because it took a lot of her time and usually led to detention, which was generally ineffective in getting the students there on time. We decided that we needed to figure out a way to get the students to class on time.

At our initial meeting, I asked Ms. Williams to pull the grades of each student. Sure enough, 16 were already failing and it was only three weeks into school. We agreed that these students already had a negative feeling about Spanish. They had probably never tasted success in this subject and were already doing poorly. For students to get to class on time and complete their work, they often have to see how it is in their best interest to do so. If kids with behavior difficulties don't believe they have a chance to succeed, they will give up.

I suggested a strategy that I learned from Bob Smith. I was fortunate enough to have Bob as my mentor early in my career. Bob was known for having complete control of his classes without resorting to meanness, threats, or hostility. The strategy Bob had taught me was to provide an academic incentive for students to get to class on time. The first step was to think about some major concepts that we were trying to teach. Ms. Williams and I decided that vocabulary was a major part of the Spanish curriculum. During a normal week, students would learn as many as 50 new vocabulary words. They were tested on these words every Friday at the beginning of class. We decided that on Monday we would tell the class that the following day they would be given 10 vocabulary words in Spanish along with the English meaning. The words would be on the overhead for the first three minutes of class. The next day (Wednesday), the class would have an open book quiz on the previous day's words. If students got to class on time on Tuesday with their notebook and pencil to copy the words, and if they brought their words to class on Wednesday, they would have an easy 100 percent quiz grade. We did this every day of the week, except Friday: On Wednesday, our students would get 10 new words and on Thursday, they would be quizzed on Tuesday's and Wednesday's words. Friday would be a closed-book quiz on all of the words from the week. If students got to class on time, copied the words, and brought their materials each day, they could earn three grades of 100 percent before the Friday closed-book quiz. It is important to remember that at this point our goal was just to get them to class on time with their materials. We were not trying to teach Spanish. That would come later.

The following week the words began. Three minutes into class the overhead went off. We made it very clear to the class that we did not want students who got to class giving their notes away. We explained that we were not going to police them, but anyone caught giving their notes to a late student would be required to take all quizzes for the entire week without notes. Conventional wisdom is that students caught giving their words away should get a zero. But Bob taught me that "top students are not willing to risk an easy 'A' so they can give some a**h**e the answers." We also explained that we were aware of who did not make it to class on time and would be looking closely at their quiz grades. The results were remarkable. On the first day we did this, five of our chronically late students showed up on time. They scurried to write down the words before the three-minute time limit expired. One of the most troubled students in class, Juan, was a 17-year-old sophomore from a tough neighborhood whose father and uncle were in jail. His mother worked three jobs and he spent most nights and mornings taking care of his seven-year-old sister. Although his family was from Puerto Rico and Spanish was his native language, he was in beginning Spanish for the third time! That's what happens when homework never gets done and a student is always late and disruptive.

Before the quizzes, Juan's class average was 55. The Tuesday that we began this experiment, he got to class on time. He forgot his pen, but because Ms. Williams was so impressed that he was there on time she gave him one of hers. He scratched the words on a torn sheet of notebook paper and delicately crumpled it into his pocket. Organizational skills were not his strength. I reminded him how important it was to bring that sheet of paper to class the following day. I was not counting on it. Sure enough, though, Juan showed up on Wednesday with the crumpled paper, which he used to get his first 100 percent of the year. He also used the same crumpled sheet of paper to write down Wednesday's words. On Thursday, Juan made it to class on time for his third straight day. His buddy, Eric, however, did not get there on time any of the days. I heard Eric ask Juan if he could borrow his notes. Juan turned around, looked at his friend, and said "Man, get your a** to class on time and take your own notes!" Ms. Williams and I were astonished! Did we both just hear Juan tell someone else to get to class on time? Wow. We were both starting to become believers.

The Friday closed-book quiz was the biggest surprise. We knew that many of the students were not going to study, and we were concerned that not doing well would cause them to give up. We also knew that we could not give them open book quizzes forever. At some point they would have to learn the words on their own. The first Friday quiz was interesting to watch. Our good students were done quickly, as always. We knew they would study and continue to do well as they had done all year. However, we noticed a drastic improvement in the attitude and energy level of our weaker students. They were taking their time trying to figure out the words. They were busy writing down answers. After class we corrected the papers with more amazement. Students who previously scored in the 50s were scoring in the 70s. Students who were scoring in the 20s were now scoring in the 50s and 60s. What Ms. Williams and I failed to realize through the entire process was that the open book quizzes were teaching Spanish better than we had done all year. Just the repetition alone for four straight days had kids remembering what many of the words meant. Although there was still a long way to go, the improvement was dramatic. By giving them an easy way to get three quiz grades of 100, we were essentially saying, "Here is your 'A.' If you decide not to keep it, don't blame us."

In retrospect, Ms. Williams and I accomplished a number of different things. We reached our goal of getting these kids to class on time. We also changed their attitudes toward Spanish. Instead of them seeing it as a subject of failure, they saw it as a place where, if they got to class on time and brought their materials, they could be successful. Finally, we accomplished the most important goal of all: we were teaching Spanish.

After two months, we made the Thursday quiz closed book as well. By this time, most of the students were doing so well that it was not a problem getting them to study for another quiz. We repeated this process for the entire year, and had only one student fail the course. Juan passed with an 88 percent average, which was easily the highest average of his academic life.

STUDENTS WHO WANT TO LOOK GOOD IN FRONT OF THEIR FRIENDS

We believe that this is the most common reason power struggles occur in school. Kids don't want to look bad in front of each other and teachers don't want to look weak in front of students. In general, it is better not to correct a behavior at all (unless danger is imminent), than to try to correct a student in front of friends. It is better to get together with the student later when there is no audience around than to try to correct misbehavior in front of an entire class. Let your students know that you won't always stop class to handle an incident of misbehavior. It doesn't mean you didn't see it, it doesn't mean you didn't hear it. It just means you think teaching is more important in that moment. Almost nothing good comes when we try to discipline students in front of their peers. Instead, we advocate meeting with whomever you have issues with later and handling things then.

Fights often occur because students don't what to look bad in front of each other. They call us names because they need to "save face." In some gang-infested schools, students will kill when made to look bad in front of their friends.

I (BDM) remember being afraid to play tackle football with the other boys in my neighborhood. When they called, my brother would run to the field to be a part of the game, but I stayed away. I never wanted to admit that I was scared, because that would lead to ridicule and teasing from the other kids, so my mom told me to blame her. She would say, "Tell them I said you can't play. I have things for you to do."

My parents understood the importance of me not looking bad in front of my friends. My mom always took the blame.

We encourage teachers to do the same. Care about keeping your students in class and getting back to teaching. Many aggressive and hostile youth have developed a reputation. When an argument occurs with them and we walk away, they will inevitably call us a name under their breath. Usually it is an exasperated "Whatever!" Try to hear this differently. Instead of the student calling you out, imagine they said this, "Mr. Smith, right now I have to call you a name under my breath. If I don't, my friends will think I'm a wimp and my reputation will get shattered. I really don't mean any disrespect by it. In fact, I really don't mean it, but I'm sure you understand that I have to be around them all day every day, including on the bus and in the cafeteria. You have no idea how they'd give it to me then if I don't say this now. If you just ignore it the argument will be over. Please be the mature adult who is getting paid and don't respond. Thanks so much."

Would you be less offended if a student said that? We believe that the above statement is really what the students are saying in the only way they know. It is so very important that we stay personally connected without taking personally what they say.

STUDENTS WHO ARE SEEKING ATTENTION

Many of our disruptive, hostile, rude, and aggressive students get little if any positive attention in their lives. They have learned to believe that any attention is better than no attention. Therefore, they disrupt the class, knowing full well we will stop our lesson to deal with them. This gives them the attention they are seeking from their classmates and from the teacher.

This reminds me (BDM) of Luis. I was teaching at a high school in downtown Buffalo, New York. It was an earth science class with 40 students, three textbooks, and hardly any running water in the science lab. It was one of those lessons that began as a disaster. You know the kind I mean: where you are teaching, but even you are confused.

I was attempting to teach a measuring unit out of the text-book. My back was to the class and I was writing on the board. Suddenly I was struck in the back of the head by a paper air-plane. Most teachers would turn around and ask who threw it. I didn't have to. Luis, about six foot one, was standing on top of a desk with his arms spread wide, staring me down. He looked hard at me and said, "Dude, you have no clue what you are doing. This lesson is a joke. This whole class is a joke. And you are the biggest joke of all." I had an important decision to make. I couldn't let the students think it is okay to talk to me like that, but remember our two main goals?

I looked at Luis and with strong eye contact and a firm tone I said to the class, "Okay everyone, take out a sheet of paper and make the best paper airplane you possibly can. Except for Luis. We all know he can make a paper airplane. Luis, I need you up here with me for this activity."

Luis: Man, I ain't coming up there.

Mr. M.:   Okay. Then who will?

Luis: Nah. I will.

Mr. M.:   (to the class, but inching toward Luis) When you are all finished making your airplanes, Luis will tell you to clear out the desks.

Luis: Yo, clear out the desks!

Mr. M.:   (now standing shoulder-to-shoulder with Luis, right in his ear) Luis, I gotta tell you, talking to me like that in front of the entire class is rude, embar-rassing, and I don't like it. I would never talk to you that way, and I trust you will never do that to me again. If you have a problem with how I'm teaching, there are other, more appropriate ways to tell me. Thanks.

Before he can respond I'm back to the class.

Mr. M: Okay. Luis, break these guys into 10 teams of four.

Luis: You over there, you over there, you over there. Let's go, we don't have all day!

Mr. M.:   On Luis's count, the first person in each group is going to throw the paper airplane. Luis will measure how far each plane goes and write the measurement on the board.

Luis: Man, I ain't writing shit.

Mr. M: Okay. Then who will?

Luis: No. I will.

A very interesting dynamic occurred here. I publicly asked Luis to do something. When he said no, I challenged him. Not by arguing, but by asking for someone to take his place. Luis was the leader of the class and craved attention, so he immediately said he'd come up front and do what I asked. He could not bear the idea of all eyes on someone else. Remember, he challenged me in front of the group, and that made him my leader. I needed him on my side if I was to have success with the rest of the class. It was easy for him to break them into groups because they respected what he said and valued his opinion. By realizing this, I saved myself a lot of energy. In the end, I accomplished my two goals: I kept him in class and I got back to teaching. I also modeled an appropriate way for him to tell me when he did not like something.

Is it ever okay to remove a student?

Many educators ask us if we believe it is ever okay to remove a student from class. They say that some students are so outrageous and so disruptive that learning is impossible for everyone else. The answer is "yes," sometimes it is appropriate to remove a student. Sometimes the needs of a student make it impossible for us to teach or for students to learn. An evening away from a spouse is not the same as a divorce. The way we remove the student must preserve the student's dignity and self-worth, however. Remember, it would have been easy to remove Luis, but—like it or not—he would be back. If at all possible, I don't want life with him to be miserable. There are two different ways to remove a student. Which sounds more familiar to you?

First removal method:

Teacher: *(usually from across the room)* Johnny, I've had it with you! I can't take the annoying behavior anymore. You know the rules and you're breaking them. Go down to the principal's office. Now!

Second removal method:

Teacher: *(as privately as possible)* Susan, right now that behavior is preventing me from teaching. I'd prefer for you to stay right here in class and learn. You are an important part of our class and I'll miss you if you choose to go. However, if you decide to continue with that annoying behavior I'm going to have to ask you to leave. If you choose to go, please come back as soon as you are ready to learn.

The first removal method invites an argument. It offers no decision-making opportunities for the student and pretty much guarantees hostility upon his or her return. The second removal method isn't really a removal. In this removal method, we ask the student to leave if she can't behave, but we encourage her to return as soon as she is able to behave. Difficult students are much less likely to take the door when the onus is placed on them. Additionally, if we are asked to defend our actions by an administrator or parent, we can very clearly show that we did not throw the student out, but in fact we asked her to stay. We even told the student that we would miss her, an act that requires professionalism.

KEY POINT FROM THE CHAPTER

We must figure out why a student is misbehaving before we can treat the behavior. Attempt to place your difficult student in one of the above categories. This will give you the platform to begin the treatment process. Remember, removal should be the last option, and kids usually come back whether we like it or not. So when removing students, be sure to offer them the door and clearly explain you will miss them if they decide to leave.

4

Fair Versus Equal

We want to restate our two main goals within the classroom. We know that when we direct our actions toward these goals, success comes our way with just about any student. Goal Number 1 is to keep the kids in class. If they are not in class, they are not learning. If they are not learning, they are falling behind. Most kids who fall behind become disruptive. Goal Number 2 is to get back to teaching. Notice that it is not one of our goals to intimidate the class. This is because we know that we will naturally look strong and authoritative and get the class's attention when we keep students there and get back to teaching.

In Chapter 2, we promised to tell you what to do so you'll never again hear your students say, "That's not fair!" Many teachers incorrectly make decisions about an individual student based on what other students in their class will say. In other words, many teachers are more concerned with the appearance than the actuality of being fair. The concept of fair versus the concept of equal is crucial when working with students with challenging behaviors. If we do not adopt and completely understand a philosophy that distinguishes between these two concepts, we put ourselves at a huge disadvantage when working with these students.

Although we have written about this concept before (Curwin & Mendler, 1999; Mendler, 2005), we would like to pose the following question: "What does it mean to be fair?" Imagine one of your students asks you that question. How do you respond? For educators, the word *fair* should mean that each student will get what he or she needs to be successful in the classroom. Now we want to pose a different question: "What does it mean to be equal?" The answer to this question is easier. *Equal* means that everyone, regardless of ability or need, is treated in the same way. We promise our students that we will always do our best to be fair, which means we often will not be treating them exactly the same way.

TEACHING "FAIR VERSUS EQUAL" TO YOUR CLASS

Teaching and explaining this concept is best accomplished on the first day of school, but can be done any time. Write the words "fair" and "equal" on the board. Then walk around your classroom and ask each student the question: "What does it mean to be fair?" Allow them to think about it for a few seconds. They may struggle with this question, which provokes good thinking and is exactly what we want. Almost always their first answer will be "fair means the same," which means that they think treating people fairly means treating everyone the same way. After each student answers, move to the next and ask the same question. Your follow-up question to them will be: "Then what does it mean to be equal? If being fair means treating everyone the same way, what does the word equal mean?"

After some discussion, clearly explain to them your definition of each one of these words. Tell your students that you will always do your best to be fair to them. This means if Kristin needs to work on writing and Fred needs to work on reading, that is what each of them will do. Being "fair" means to do what each student needs. They can tell you it is not equal, but you never promised to be equal. If you or your students are still confused about these two words, use these examples:

- Example 1: If two people order a pizza with ten slices, how many slices is it fair for each person to get? Most people say five, which illustrates why this concept is so important and needs to be taught. *Equal* means that both eat exactly the same amount, or five slices each. *Fair* means that both eat until they are satisfied. If one person eats three and is full, it would be outrageous for that person to eat two more pieces in the name of fairness.

- Example 2: Point to seven students and ask them to pretend that they each have a headache. Just as they all have the same teacher in school, ask them to pretend that they all have the same doctor. These seven students go into the doctor's office. On the wall in the doctor's office is a sign that says "For headaches, give Advil." The doctor prescribes Advil for Students 1 through 6. Thinking nothing of it, these six students go home, take the Advil, and lose their headaches. However, Student 7 goes into the doctor's office and explains that he is allergic to Advil. The doctor looks at the student and says, "But that is what we have here." Student 7 answers, "I am different from the other patients. I can't have Advil. Advil doesn't work for me." To which the doctor again responds, "That's what we do here. Our policy says that when someone has a headache we give Advil. And besides, if I don't give you Advil, it wouldn't be fair to patients 1 to 6, now would it?" This type of response would be ridiculous and outrageous from a doctor. Make sure that the students understand that the doctor is demonstrating the concept of equal but not of fair.

- Other examples: Discuss or assign students to write about times or situations at home in which brothers or sisters were treated differently and it was fair. Examples include allowance, bedtime, chores, and activities. Discuss the results with your class, stressing that in class you will always treat them fairly but sometimes treat them differently from each other.

Putting the Concept of Fair Into Classroom Action

Can you imagine doctors making a decision about a patient based on what they did for the last patient? It would be totally ridiculous, yet in school we frequently do this. School policy and practice needs to be based on giving proper assignments or consequences based on what will best teach each student. Here is sample dialogue about how to put this most important concept to work in the classroom.

Begin by teaching the concept to your students in the manner described above. Even after the best explanation, it invariably occurs that one or more students complain when you give a different homework assignment or consequence. When this occurs, the response needs to be as follows:

Teacher: What is the problem with the consequence I gave you?

Student: Joe and I broke the same rule, but you gave me a detention and you are only calling his mom. No way is that fair.

Teacher: I am not willing to discuss the consequence I gave Joe because that is about him, not about you. However, if you have a problem with your consequence I would be happy to discuss it.

Too many students are so conditioned to point out what other kids are getting that they don't know how to look internally. We learn to take responsibility by looking inside ourselves, not by comparing ourselves to others. Do not discuss details about one student with others unless there is a valuable lesson for others to learn. (Keep in mind that there is also the important issue of confidentiality, which often has legal implications.)

Teacher: So, is there a problem with the consequence I gave you?

Student: Well, it is ridiculous. No way should I have a detention.

Teacher: Maybe not. Then convince me of something that would work better so this problem doesn't occur again.

Student: I think you should call home and talk to my mom.

Teacher: So are you telling me that all I have to do is call your mom tonight and starting tomorrow I will get better behavior?

Students now have three different responses that they can pick from: "Yes," "No," or most commonly, "I don't know." We will start with the first possible response.

Teacher: So, you're telling me that all I have to do is call your mom and starting tomorrow you will behave yourself in this class?

Student: Yes, that is what I'm saying.

Teacher: Okay. I'm sorry. I had no idea that all I had to do was call your mom. What time is she going to be home? If I am able to speak with her, this detention will be shredded.

Student: Okay, she'll be home by 7:00 pm.

Teacher: I will call your mom tonight around 7:00. If I talk to her you can consider this detention gone. If not, I'll see you after school tomorrow. Sound good?

Student: I guess.

Teacher: You guess? Because if the phone call isn't going to work, maybe something else will.

Please understand that, as educators, we do not care about the consequence. All we care about is improved behavior. Too often, educators get so caught up in the consequence that we forget it is merely a vehicle we use to arrive at a destination. The destination is better behavior, and that is not negotiable. How we get there is based on what will best work for that individual. There are even times when we prefer the student to decide on the consequence.

The second option is for the student to reply "I don't know" to the question. In that case, the following sequence is recommended:

Teacher: So you're telling me that all I have to do is call your mom and starting tomorrow I can get better behavior from you?

Student: Um, I don't know. I'm not sure.

Teacher: Well, here's the thing. Until you come up with something that you think will work better, I have to do what I think is going to be most effective. But if you think of something between now and the end of the day, I'll be glad to listen. Until that time, the detention is what it is going to be. But remember, I want to know if you have a better idea. Hope to hear from you.

Here we are leaving the door open for the student to show some responsibility and accountability to create what is going to work for him. If he cannot give us a better consequence, then we need to do what we think will work best.

The final possible response to the question is "No."

Teacher: So you're telling me that all I have to do is call your mom and starting tomorrow I can get better behavior from you?

Student: No, I'm not saying that.

Teacher: Thanks for being honest. If you are telling me a phone call home is not going to work, why would I do it? I am going to stick with the detention unless you can suggest something that you think will really work better.

Implementing how to be fair and not worrying about treating everyone exactly the same way is vital in a successful classroom. Students learn at different rates and may not all be capable of the same performance. This holds true with grades and homework, as well. Two friends, Leah and Jasmine, were students in my (BDM's) class. Leah missed a ton of school due to many personal problems, and as a result, she failed math for the quarter. Based on her attendance and performance, her actual grade was a 40 percent but I gave her a 60 percent. My goal was to keep some hope alive. A grade of 40 percent would have given her no hope of passing the year. I gave her a 60 percent knowing that all she needed was to achieve a 70 percent the next quarter to pass for the year. I considered that grade attainable for her with adequate work and effort.

Jasmine, on the other hand, came to school every day. She hardly did any work and was loud, rude, and disruptive in class. She barely passed with a 65 percent, and was furious when she found out Leah's grade was only 5 points lower. She angrily confronted me about this:

Jasmine: She never even came to class, and I only got 5 points higher than her? No way is that fair.

Mr. M.:   You sound angry and we can talk about your grade if you want, but I am not going to discuss Leah's grade with you. That's about her. What's the problem with your 65?

Jasmine: But Leah got . . .

Mr. M.:   (cutting her off) I know what she got. I'm the one who gave it to her. What's the problem with *your* 65? Last I checked, you hardly did any work yourself and you are entirely capable of doing much better in this class. I will not accept anything less than your best effort, nor should you. When you are ready to talk about *you* I'll be glad to listen.

It is then important to walk away until the student is ready to discuss himself or herself.

Explaining "Fair" to Parents

Discussing the concept of fair is one good way to introduce yourself and what you value during parent-teacher night. Let parents know that you value success and responsibility for each of your students. The following points can be used to guide your discussion:

Greet your students' parents by telling them at least one good thing about each student in the class.

Thank them for coming.

Begin your presentation by having the words "Fair" and "Equal" written on the board.

Tell parents that they are about to participate in an activity that will show them the way your class is going to work.

Ask the parents, "What does it mean to be fair?" Let some of them take a chance and attempt to define what that word means to them. Most parents will include the word "equal" in their definition.

After getting their responses, give them your definition: "In this class, the word *fair* means that every individual will get what he or she needs to be successful, to the best of my ability as a teacher." Be sure to emphasize the word "individual."

Repeat these steps with the word "equal."

This definition will be much easier for parents to define, and they will probably give you an answer such as, "*Equal* means 'the same.'"

Write the definition of each word on the board so all can see.

Tell parents that you will always do your best to be fair to each child. This means you will not always be treating them exactly the same way.

Explain that this means sometimes their son or daughter might get different homework or a different consequence than someone else in the class.

If you need an example to help them understand your logic, use the pizza or doctor's office example.

It is also important to make it very clear to parents that you will not be discussing anyone else's child with them. This will keep them from complaining about what you are doing for others.

I (BDM) have done this in my classroom for several years. Parents love it. Every year at least one parent raises a hand and asks, "Are you telling us there are teachers that don't operate this way? Are you saying that there are teachers who actually know some students read at a first-grade level but force them to read at a fifth-grade level because that's what everyone else is doing?" My response to them is the same as it is to kids when they talk about other students. "It is not for me to say how other teachers run their classrooms. You'll have to ask them if you want to know. I just want to let you know how this classroom works." Talking about other teachers is another losing battle.

The final element in this chapter is about rewarding kids once they are able to talk about themselves. It is a lot of work for many of them to accomplish this.

Student: I don't think it is a good idea for me to serve my detention tonight.

Mr. M: Okay. Why not?

Student: Because tonight I have my grandmother's birthday party, then I have hockey practice, and I just don't have time tonight.

Mr. M: Is tomorrow better?

Student: Yes.

Mr. M: Okay. I'll see you then instead!

If the teacher does not occasionally give the students what they are asking for, he learns that the effort put into talking only about himself is not worth it. But if the teacher listens and even gives the students what they are asking for, he learns it is worth it next time.

The concept of fair versus equal enables us to give each student what he or she needs to be successful. Be sure to explain to your class early in the year: "Being fair means each of you get what you need. Being equal means each of you gets exactly the same thing. Do not complain to me that I'm not being fair when I give different assignments or different homework. You can complain that it's not equal but remember, I'm not promising to be equal in here, I'm promising to be fair."

KEY POINTS FROM THE CHAPTER

Fair vs. Equal is one of the most important concepts to learn and understand for successful classroom management. Here are the key points to remember.

1. Tell your students you will always do your best to be fair to each and every one of them, which means you will not always treat them exactly the same way.

2. Tell your students you will only talk to them about themselves. You will not talk to them about anyone else in the class.

3. Let them know that they can always talk to you about problems; however, you are never interested in their opinion of what you're doing for someone else.

4. Be sure to clearly post the definition of each word. *Fair*: Every individual gets what he or she needs to be successful. *Equal*: Everyone gets exactly the same thing.

5. Don't be afraid to teach this concept by using the doctor's office and pizza examples we used earlier in the chapter.

6. Let your class know ahead of time how you will respond to them if they complain about someone else, i.e. "What's the problem with what I did for you?"

7. Let parents know ahead of time that you will always do your best to be fair to each of their children, which means you will not be treating them exactly the same way.

8. Tell parents you will never discuss their child with another parent, which is why you will not discuss other children with them. Let parents know very clearly that you will always talk to them about their child and do what you think is in their child's best interest.

9. Listen to students and their parents. If they suggest consequences or homework assignments that they think are better than the ones you've assigned, feel free to use them.

10. Remember, homework and consequences should be viewed as vehicles to a destination. The destination should not be negotiable (You will behave. You will learn how to multiply. You will understand how to write a sentence). Be flexible with the vehicle. Allow students to have a say in what they think is going to work best for them. With ownership comes responsibility. Follow the steps in Chapter Four and you will be on the road to having a well-managed classroom.

5

Classroom Strategies for the Teacher

I n this chapter, we focus on specific classroom strategies that can make a difference with students who have behavior difficulties. Many problems in school have their roots firmly planted outside the classroom, but for now we want to focus on you, the teacher. What can you do in your classroom to be successful with your students? How can you get them to listen without telling them to listen? How can you get them to quiet down without telling them to quiet down? How can you get them to ask thoughtful questions without telling them to ask thoughtful questions?

Great teachers have proven that great lessons are the great equalizer. A stimulating lesson will engage students with even the most disruptive behavior. We will share examples of dynamic and engaging lessons that can involve every student. These are ideas that come from educators all over the world that you can mold to fit your individual classroom and your individual students.

This chapter is divided into three parts: Part 1 suggests numerous strategies to build effective relationships with students and explains how to sustain these relationships even during difficult moments. The best way to prevent a behavior problem is to engage students with lessons that are interesting and entertaining. Part 2 offers many examples to make that engagement happen by teaching great lessons. Part 3 provides a number of strategies that show how to best assign material and assess performance so that students who are at risk of failure remain hopeful and motivated.

PART 1: STRATEGIES FOR BUILDING AND SUSTAINING RELATIONSHIPS

I (BDM) was standing at my classroom door while saying good morning to students arriving for class, when around the corner came my new student, Abby, her high heels leaving marks on the polished floor. She looked me up and down, her chin hitting the top of her chest, and the back of her head hitting the back of her neck with each movement. Her arms were crossed, and with a low, nasty tone she said, "I just want to let you know that I'm not doing a f***ing thing this year." Abby then brushed my shoulder with hers, charged into the room, and slammed herself down at a desk. The desk tipped back and forth, almost tipping over, before settling into place with a bang. As difficult as it was at that moment, I walked up to her, put out my hand, looked her in the eye and said, "Nice to meet you, Abby." I then got out of there quickly, because if I had stuck around Abby might think I was being disingenuous and decide to engage me in a power struggle that I was not interested in having. However, I had to try to like her and convey caring so that each day might be less of a struggle. Abby was now a part of my class and I was required to teach her. After Abby charged into the room, I had a decision to make. Although it was not okay for anyone to talk or act toward me the way Abby did (especially not in front of the rest of the class), I had to keep my eye on the ball and keep my two goals front and center: keep kids in class and get back to teaching.

A major reason for working at developing and sustaining positive relationships is to prevent these moments from occurring. When they do, though, all of our students need to know that we will effectively handle things in due time while remaining in control. Students learn that we will deal with their attitude and behavior at a calmer time so that their dignities and ours are preserved.

Little things really matter

With so many students lonely and craving a sense of belonging, it is often the small basic human elements that make the big differences. Good teachers have always done things to make their classrooms welcoming. Many teachers greet students as they come in the room, calling them by name, or simply saying hello with a warm smile. Although simple, these are the kinds of practices that create warmth for all students.

Warmth is an elusive concept, one that is hard to define with words but easy to recognize when it is present. For students, warmth can best be described in terms of the school being a place where they are respected and loved. Who they are and how hard they try is valued more than what they know. Warmth exists when the development of policies and practices is guided by the question, "How will this improve students' lives?"

At a recent seminar at a suburban high school, a 23-year veteran teacher challenged the idea of his school becoming more student centered. He said, "This school belongs to us [teachers], because we'll be here long after they [students] leave. They are visitors here for a few years, and then they are gone. They need to conform to our expectations." Although this colleague's skills and talents are important, he has missed a core issue. Without him, the school would continue to exist. Without students, it would not!

Always remember, "School is for kids," for all kids, including those we find unattractive, those who misbehave, and those who don't give their best. It is our professional duty to welcome and teach each student with enthusiasm, care, and courage. To do less diminishes us and all of society.

Without doubt, it takes a deep commitment to fight the temptation to turn away and not engage those students who seem unpredictable, weird, or aggressive toward themselves or others. A friend recently related an incident where she saw a boy in the hall of the high school where she teaches banging his head repetitively against a locker. Two nearby teachers pretended not to see this worrisome moment. They were understandably afraid and uncertain. Having been trained to work with difficult youth, my friend approached the boy, got close to him, and told him, "Wow, how terrible the day must be for you. But you can stop hurting yourself now, and then we'll start figuring out what to do next." When she reached out her hand to his, he stopped, acknowledging his inner turmoil. Later, when she asked one of her colleagues why he simply walked past the boy, she was at first told, "The kid is crazy, and that isn't my job!" The same colleague later confessed to being afraid of approaching the boy.

It is important that we confront our fears and, when necessary, develop the skills that help us know what to do in difficult situations. When I (ANM) first began working at a facility with juvenile delinquents who were incarcerated—some of them for committing violent crimes—a part of me was terrified. There were times I met one-on-one with a youth in a secured room with nobody else around. I found myself doing things to befriend the residents, ostensibly to develop rapport in my role as a psychologist. That was, of course, necessary and okay, but I could also hear the voice of my fear from within motivating each of my moves. I was essentially unable to engage the children's fears and anxieties because I was afraid that they might lose control of themselves and hurt me. It was only when I confronted myself honestly, and after I took some self-defense training (that, incidentally, I never needed to use) that I felt confident to really be myself and reach out without fear.

When we are afraid of our students, it takes courage to acknowledge the fear and then develop a plan that increases self-confidence. Students who have challenging behavior need confident teachers who know what to do when control is an issue. It is when this confidence is in place that our strategies of warmth are especially effective.

Greet your students

Make it an everyday practice to say hello to each one as the students arrive in your classroom. If that frequency is unrealistic, then greet each child no less than twice each week. Welcome them as they arrive. Convey the attitude that your classroom is equally their classroom and you are welcoming them home. Students really appreciate thoughtful gestures from their teachers like a greeting card, a birthday card, or a "Good job!" note, but a welcoming smile can be just as effective. Standing at the door and greeting our students is a good strategy for building relationships. It gives us the opportunity to make a quick personal connection in a relatively private way. Students are much more likely to respond to personal questions when they are posed in a nonthreatening way and when no one else hears the question or the answer. I (BDM) knew this was where I had to begin with Abby. Her success was going to come before class, after class, and in the hallway. She had to see that I cared about her before she would perform well academically. Rather than scurrying about getting papers in place while students are arriving to class, greeting them at the door shows them that we are prepared, in charge, and well organized—traits we want to encourage in them.

Notice and build on students' strengths

Building relationships is also about noticing and asking the right questions so we become more aware of factors affecting our students. Abby wore too much makeup, her shirt and skirt were too tight, and she had an unattractive complexion. Knowing that most adolescent girls strongly value their appearance, it wasn't much of a stretch to realize that Abby was probably feeling miserable about herself. Probing a bit, I also learned that she had recently moved a thousand miles when she had been kicked out of her uncle's house, her father wanted no part of her, she had no mother, and she was currently living with a foster family in a run-down house. This was probably a student with little support who had nobody that thought of her as special in any way. The goal was to find something that she liked so I could build on it.

The opportunity to find that special thing happened by chance during her second week in class. It was Tuesday morning and Abby walked into class as she always did: without a pen, her homework, or any interest in being there! However, she usually carried a notebook, and this time she dropped it and out came a flood of drawings. The detail and shading were amazing. I looked closely at them before returning her notebook. Now I had something. The next day as Abby walked in, I commented on her drawings. She said she loved to draw, that it was her passion. Shortly thereafter I introduced her to the art teacher. Her love for art was obvious, and she became one of the best students in the drawing class. Although Abby had not yet become academically engaged in my class, I knew if I kept building the relationship I could teach her anything she needed to know.

Out of frustration, educators sometimes tell disengaged students that if they're not willing to do the work or pay attention in class, they need to find somewhere else to be. Sometimes educators have to choose the best from a few bad choices: We usually prefer for students to remain with us rather than leave, unless they are being so disruptive that it becomes impossible for us to teach or our other students to learn. Not only does their remaining in the classroom provide a chance that they will hear something important we are teaching, it gives us more opportunity to discover quiet strengths like Abby's that we might otherwise miss.

Tell personal stories

Kids love hearing stories about their teachers. Relating a personal story to an actual lesson can be very effective. For example, a history teacher we know told a story about his time fighting in the Vietnam War. He had riveting pictures of weapons, wounded soldiers, and of the enemy. He had the complete attention of his students during these classes.

Jan Freeman, a paraprofessional in Jackson, Mississippi, used her hobby as a way to connect with students. One of

Jan's goals was to visit and spend at least three days in each of the 50 states. Jan took pictures of historical landmarks, ate in local mom-and-pop restaurants, and stayed in locally owned hotels. She then created a scrapbook of her travels and shared them with her students. Her students help plan the trips by researching different states, important historical sites, and the best local places to eat and sleep.

Jen Hall, a teacher in Phoenix, Arizona, shared an activity she uses on the first day of school. She asks students to write down their favorite sport, video game, and music artist. She then does the same thing and shares her answers with the class, which enables her to connect with her students on the first day of school. Her kids share their answers with the class, too, making the classroom a place where students realize that their interests matter.

Call students by name

Learn your students' names early and use them often. People are impressed when you know their names, and they feel good when you convey some personal knowledge about them. Furthermore, it is much easier to command respect during tough moments when you know a student's name.

Several teachers have asked for advice about what to do with students who act inappropriately in the hallways between classes. Often they will preface their question by asking for advice in disciplining students they don't know. Our advice is simple: Walk up to the student and introduce yourself.

Mr. Grant: Excuse me, I'm not sure we've met. My name is Mr. Grant. I'm a science teacher here. What is your name?

Student: Kara.

Mr. Grant: Nice to meet you, Kara. Can you do me a favor and please pick up that piece of paper you just dropped? I'd really appreciate it. By the way, that's a really cool sweater you are wearing. Where did you get it?

Approaching students, introducing yourself, and then asking them to stop the inappropriate behavior is often much more effective than just asking them to stop.

Know who your students are

We mentioned earlier how important it is to know your students' interests, perceived strengths, weaknesses, likes, and dislikes. In this way, you can connect with them before frustration leads to withdrawal or aggression. Interest inventories, student surveys, and incomplete sentence forms can elicit a wealth of helpful information in a nonthreatening manner. Be aware, though, that some parents (and some students) may consider this a violation of privacy. Should that be an issue, simply hand out an index card and ask students to write down what makes it hard for them to learn and what helps them learn. By limiting the query to learning, privacy issues are fully respected.

Teach empathy

The best way of building a sense of community among all students is to model and encourage displays of empathy in the classroom. One of the most powerful things an educator can do is simple, but requires courage: apologize if you make a mistake. When we blow it and know it, an apology expresses genuine remorse that is essential to the development of conscience and empathy.

A high school teacher, Mr. Aziz, recently shared his graphic "My I" strategy that he uses with his class. This strategy is a variation of the "I am lovable and capable" strategy developed by Sidney B. Simon. Each week, Mr. Aziz draws a full body self-portrait and pins it to his shirt. The words "My I" are written on the portrait to convey ownership as he lets his students know that words and deeds can either be supportive or disrespectful. When his students say or do things to him that he considers disrespectful, he takes a scissors and cuts off a body part to note injury. His original goal was to get through a week with at least one body part remaining. Four weeks into this practice, improvement was so dramatic that on average only two body parts each week were trimmed.

The concrete symbol of a person being cut served as a powerful point of awareness and source of learning. It became common for students to ask him what they had done when he cut off a body part. He learned that most of the time his students did not intend disrespect. Their statements reflected the "in your face" society so prevalent today in the United States and in much of the Western world.

An elementary teacher we met models patience with her young children by writing the word *P A T I E N C E* on the chalkboard each day. She teaches the virtue of showing patience as well as the frustration we feel and the time we lose when we act in ways that upset people's patience. She explained that when things happened in class that challenged her patience, she would erase one letter. Letters left at the end of the day were traded for extra play activities as both a token of appreciation and consequence of thoughtfulness.

A kindergarten teacher, Cindy Amos, told the five-year-olds she works with to "smell the flowers and blow out the candles" when they are upset. By doing this they learn that taking deep breaths can help calm them down. This idea is great for children of any age. It works for adults, too.

One way to build empathy among students is to have them create an "I'm good at" board. All students write down one or two things that they believe they are good at. The students have names posted on the board and the things they are good at below their name. When students have a question, concern, or problem, they are required to check the board for another student who could help before asking the teacher. Students get to know each other, and benefit from each other as helpers. Students can use individual strengths to make their classroom a better place.

We can teach empathy by placing students who seem not to care about others in positions to help either people or pets. At first these students need to be supervised because kids who have been emotionally wounded and abused frequently lack empathy. They have shut down to people as a means of protection. They also may harbor resentment for the hurts they have experienced, and are therefore at greater risk of hurting or abusing others. Many hurting students are reawakened to empathy through supervised experiences in which caring is requisite. For example, I (ANM) worked with juvenile delinquent youth who became actual clowns and then entertained children at nursery schools and seniors at a nursing home. Many of these boys became more sensitive through this experience, because they realized the positive effects their behavior could have on others. We have seen street-toughened kids make excellent mentors for severely disabled children and the elderly. We have observed youth who have difficult, oppositional behaviors who are placed as mentors willingly performing such basic functions as feeding an infant and even changing diapers. At school, students with challenging behavior can be offered supervised opportunities in which they help a younger child in need.

Through the years, Dan was feared by many as an explosive, aggressive, hostile student who lacked empathy for others. Dan was a gang member, and often talked of brutal fights he had witnessed or in which he had participated. By most accounts, Dan was a kid that you would want to keep far away from young, impressionable youth. However, I (BDM) decided to let him get involved in the work-study program at my school. His job was to help tutor elementary students who ranged in age from seven to ten in an afterschool setting. Dan was in charge of two younger students. At first the tutoring sessions were supervised. However, after about three weeks, the parents of these two younger students asked if Dan would mentor them without supervision. They said they trusted him completely and were impressed with the impression he had made on their children. They believed their kids could not completely tell Dan their problems if the supervisor was always around. I agreed to give them 15 minutes of alone time each day with Dan. Both younger students made tremendous gains in their academic performance, with their teachers reporting much better behavior. Referrals went down. Dan also improved: his behavior improved, and his effort became more evident with regard to homework. He talked less about the trouble he got into, and more of the job he was a part of. He would beam when teachers complimented him on his work at the elementary school. Dan began seeking ways to stay after school and to come in early for extra help. The turn-around was amazing.

Let them see who you are

Students who are turned off to school and are at higher risk of doing harm often have very negative associations with school. For them, teachers are authority figures against whom they rebel. They often ignore or greet high achievement peers in a disdainful way. We need to generate a different mental picture of school so they come to see this part of their lives as important and meaningful.

Go to an event when it is likely that one of your students will be present, and greet him or her personally. Identify one or two students who usually make themselves unattractive to you and make a commitment to interact with them in a personal manner for two minutes each day for two consecutive weeks. Acknowledging birthdays and asking about a special piece of clothing or jewelry also helps change a student's point of view.

Call high-risk students at home to discuss an issue or to just ask how they are doing. Often, conflict situations can be resolved in this manner. We send a strong signal of respect and significance when we think highly enough about a student to take our own personal time to call. The message is powerful and often transforms students' perceptions when they hear such statements as, "Joe, I was upset in class today and I thought this might be a good time for us to put our heads together and come up with a solution that will work for both of us." Or, "Mike, threatening to cut up my tires tells me that you are extremely mad. Although I've thought about reporting this to the police, what I really want is for you to help me understand what I did that made you so upset. I thought this would be a good time to talk it over."

There is both safety and intimacy over the phone. The phone provides a safe barrier for students who need distance or who present in a physically threatening manner. The teacher is able to get within earshot of a student who otherwise may react negatively to close proximity. Finally, the phone provides privacy. There are no other students to attract through inappropriate behavior or who are around to comment on the interaction.

Building relationships is the golden key to success with all students. Students will work harder when they are working hard for a person they care about. Become that person first, and the content will soon follow.

Listen, listen, and then listen some more

Most problems that interfere with learning would never occur if each student had at least one important adult in his or her life who regularly listened with caring and concern and without judgment. If every child had 10 minutes a day with this caring adult who listened to recountings of victories, defeats, joys, and hurts, the power of connection would override most other factors.

We cannot provide a listener for all students to the extent that it is needed, but we can offer our willingness to connect by noticing the realities that our students face. All that may be needed is a tone of concern expressed to a student who walks in with a grumpy face. For example, if you see a grumpy student, asking how things are going with a caring, concerned voice lets him know that he is not alone.

Some children and teenagers do better when they can write down their joys and frustrations and share them with someone who cares. In the classroom, there are many small ways to accomplish this. Put out a suggestion box and invite students to offer ways to make the class a more satisfying place. Assure them that you will either implement their suggestions or tell them why you will not or can not. All suggestions that are signed can be treated in this way. To avoid silly or offensive suggestions, give students language parameters that they must respect. Any unsigned suggestions may or may not warrant feedback. Set aside time to answer the perennial question, "Why do we need to know that?" Invite older students to keep a journal; invite younger students to use art to record their feelings.

A middle school teacher in one of my (RLC's) consulting sessions recently shared her strategy of offering all students "two days off' each semester. If she detects that a student is agitated, overwhelmed, or burned out, she suggests a day off. A student may request a day off when he or she believes it's needed. The student remains in class and is expected to be nondisruptive but is not required to actively participate.

Tommy Smith, a middle school teacher in Orlando, Florida, has a "baggage box" in his classroom. He explains to students that everyone carries baggage (problems) and that from time to time this baggage may be so heavy that it gets in the way of learning and concentrating. When students bring their baggage to class, he encourages them to anonymously write about what is bugging them, place it in a sealed envelope, and put it in the box. At the end of class, students may reclaim their baggage or leave it. All old baggage is discarded at the end of the day. Many students take advantage of leaving their baggage behind. Those who want to reclaim their baggage put a symbol on the outside of the sealed envelope to denote ownership. To assure privacy, if they want it back, they must show the symbol they used on a separate paper to Mr. Smith, who then retrieves the envelope. It is rare for students to reclaim their note.

Have fun

Sometimes educators say things like, "I'm not here for that kid to like my subject or me; I'm here to teach." We agree. We are not here for students to like us, but isn't it easier for students to learn when they do like us? Don't they listen better when they are enjoying something? Don't you?

When recently polled, 300 high school students were asked the question, "What makes a good teacher?" Two hundred and twenty of their answers included the word "fun." When students view the content and the teacher as enjoyable to be around, there is usually an increase in learning and a decrease in disruptive behavior. For years, there has been a growing body of research indicating that fun, creativity, and interaction lead to or are part of high classroom achievement. Robinson and Kakela (2006) noted that bringing in guest speakers, taking students on field trips, and using playful and interactive strategies are strong motivational devices for reluctant learners. Mendler (2005) identified the power of humor to defuse power struggles and enhance learning. With so much anger and depression in the lives of children, school can become a refuge where escape into fun is an important part of the planned experience.

Allow yourself to laugh, and permit your students to enjoy being with you and each other. Every educator ought to do at least one planned enjoyable activity with every class each day.

Use nonverbal messages

Donna Rogner, a first-grade teacher in Chicago, developed a policy that she called "H or H." She told her children that each day when they entered the room they could have either a hug or a handshake. They could decide and then tell her. Ms. Rogner reported that this method was highly effective in getting the day started in the right frame of mind for her group of children with serious behavior problems. We recently met a tenth-grade high school history teacher who tried this method with one of his students. He privately reported that the student loved it. The teacher found this to be a wonderful method to use occasionally (two to three times each month), and he added that if too much time passes, some students will seek him out privately and ask if today will be an "H or H" day.

Since this colleague's experience, we have been challenging middle school and high school teachers to create techniques like this within their own zones of comfort. Most are amazed at their students' receptivity and responsiveness. Sadly, there has recently been a spike in inappropriate relations between teachers and students. Use your judgment. Instead of a hug or handshake you might give the students a choice between a handshake or a high five.

Say "no" respectfully

How we say things is usually more important than what we say. Some years ago, during an especially tight fiscal time, I (ANM) worked with a personnel director in a school district who had the unenviable task of telling teachers that they were being laid off. It was remarkable that this man's caring manner and supportive words had these very teachers extolling his virtues after he broke the news.

In any classroom, part of the job of the teacher is to say "no." When we say "no," it is important that we maintain the dignity of the student to protect our relationship with the child and to sustain the student's motivation. Simply saying "no" and offering your best reason in a concise manner is effective and appreciated: If I said "yes" or allowed an inappropriate situation to continue, I wouldn't be doing my job. My job is to make sure that we respect each other and cooperate together. Most kids usually follow up the answer "no" with the question, "Why not"? If our only response is, "Because I said so" or "It's the rule" or "It's always been done that way," we are inviting an argument. We should have reasons when we say "no," and the reasons should make sense even if students disagree. Parents do this all the time. They tell their child that bedtime is 8 o'clock. The kid occasionally goes to bed kicking and screaming, but eventually falls asleep. The kicking and screaming isn't easy to deal with, but soon the child learns that yelling isn't going to work, so the yelling stops.

FINAL QUESTIONS AND SUGGESTIONS

Since there are many ways to build warmth in your school, the key is to identify practices that are compatible with you as an individual. By connecting the practice with your style, the result is genuineness. Below are some questions and suggestions to help you get clear about what you want to do.

1. When people visit your home, what are some things you do to help them feel welcome? How can you greet your students in the same sort of way?

2. What teachers did you have when you were in school that made you feel special or important? What did they do that gave you that feeling?

3. How much class time do you take to learn about your students' lives? Take the same number of minutes learning about them as you do dealing with disruptive behaviors.

4. Think of one or two students you currently have who you find behaviorally unattractive. Are you willing to devote a significant five to ten minutes each day for as many weeks as it takes in an effort to develop a more meaningful relationship?

5. Which teachers at your school seem able to most easily connect with their students? What do they seem to do? Do you network with other teachers, watch them work, and ask them questions? Try identifying practices that you see them doing that you consider to be good ways of building and sustaining relationships.

6. Find the leaders. Think of one or two students you currently have who create problems in the classroom

and who appear to be of relatively high influence in the eyes of their peers. These students are often effective at influencing others to join their behaviors. If we can get the leaders on our side, classroom success will follow.

PART 2: STRATEGIES FOR TEACHING GREAT LESSONS

Teach to diverse learning styles and multiple intelligences

With his theory of multiple intelligences, Howard Gardner (1983) postulated the existence of seven distinct intelligences. He claimed that only two of these were highlighted in school. Those with high linguistic (word analysis and usage) or logical-math intelligence (logical reasoning) tend to do very well because schools usually emphasize these areas. In contrast, students with high bodily (kinesthetic) and musical intelligence tend to get into trouble more often because of their need for movement. For example, we tend to assume that the pencil tapper or rapper is being disruptive rather than viewing this student as needing, feeling, or expressing an inner rhythm. By expanding the definition of what constitutes intelligence, more students will be included in the learning process and school can become a less frustrating place. Gardner (1999) described "naturalistic" intelligence: the ability to recognize, sort, and find patterns in things like plants, animals, clouds, and rocks. Gardner has shown how his theory can be applied daily in the classroom for students who learn in multiple ways. Still, it is remarkable to note how so many educators persist in a one-size-fits-all style of instruction that unfortunately has dire learning consequences for those students who don't fit.

We often ask teachers who attend our seminars to think back to a class that they found difficult as students. They knew that the subject being taught was not a strength, but they had to be there anyway. We then ask these same educators to imagine that their entire school experience existed in that class and that all future classes would be similar. These images are usually sufficient to help colleagues feel how it is to be in a place where expectations don't match strengths.

We would do well to incorporate into our daily curriculums learning experiences based on what students have told us they find motivating. Among the practical approaches most students find motivating are interviewing people, making collections of things related to concepts presented in the classroom, going on field trips that integrate actual and academic experiences, working on projects with peers, acting things out, listening to guest speakers, and conducting independent experiments. Teaching to student needs and interests (differentiated instruction) has been proven successful. Tomlinson (2005) noted that teachers must differentiate their instruction so the success of all students can be attained. She went on to ask rhetorically if a student can realistically master a seventh-grade spelling list if his or her spelling skills hover at a third-grade level. Tomlinson pointed out that teachers must be willing to use graphic organizers, reading materials at different levels of complexity, and small group direct instruction. She went on to "explain" that students learn best when their interests are linked to desired educational outcomes.

Some might read Tomlinson's (2005) suggestions and wonder how it is possible to differentiate instruction for 25 different students. Fortunately, we don't have to. Most students in a class read, write, and do math at about the same level. What Tomlinson, Marzano (2003), and many other educational experts are asking is for us not to leave behind the few who need to be taught in a different way. To achieve desired outcomes, teachers must spend extra time preparing individual lessons for students who are not exactly at grade level. This takes extra time, energy, and effort. The extra work will pay off with improved student performance and better classroom behavior.

Teach with energy and enthusiasm

Any class or subject can be motivating. The way it is taught usually determines its motivational value. Teachers who love what they teach will teach it with passion, making it difficult for students to disrupt or zone out. We must remind ourselves on a daily basis why we teach and what we want to derive from it. When it is all over on retirement day, do we want students to remember us because we had the best rubrics? Do we prefer that our legacy be that we were the loudest complainer in the faculty lounge who continually detailed all the reasons we couldn't make a difference? Or do we want to be remembered as someone who ignited a passion for learning by modeling it? Remember, the best teachers teach because they want to change the lives of their students forever.

Great lessons begin by understanding outcomes

Ask yourself the following questions before starting a lesson: "What am I trying to teach? By the end of class what do I expect my students to know?" When a lesson goes poorly, it is often for two reasons: because we aren't sure of what the outcome is supposed to be or because the goals were too broad (for instance, improving reading or writing skills). If we are not sure what we are specifically trying to teach, then how can we recognize success? A good strategy is to write on the board what you want the outcome of a lesson to be. For example, at the end of this lesson students will know how to write a complete sentence. Or, at the end of this lesson, students will know how to set up and solve a two-digit subtraction problem. Success is easier to recognize when the goals of the lesson are clear. When goals are clear, a day that felt bad because someone misbehaved and the lesson didn't go exactly as planned might actually have been a success. The flip side is that without clear goals, it is possible to play a game while having fun and feeling good with our students who are learning nothing. Identifying the goals of the lesson can make it come alive and give our students and us something to strive for. It also helps organize the group as a whole and is a concrete measure of progress on a daily basis. It is important to have a reason and a purpose for everything we do in the classroom. Our decisions will not always be correct, and there will occasionally be students who are confused. But if we have an outcome that is clearly defined, usually our students will strive for the outcome we have presented.

Use these ideas for making lessons great

The effectiveness of many instructional moments depends on how well students can work together. This is especially true during cooperative learning activities. Some students believe that the word "group" is a license to disrupt. When groups are well organized and well run, there is often no better form of learning. However, kids often use this time to catch up on the latest television shows, sporting events, and gossip. There are a few essential ingredients to ensure smoothly run groups inside the classroom. When assigning students to work in groups within the classroom, the following guidelines can be helpful:

Groups should have no more than five members. Four is ideal, but five is acceptable. Six or more is a recipe for group disaster.

Put them into their groups. Once they are in the groups, have them number themselves one through four (or one through five, depending on the number of kids in each group). Students should not be allowed to choose their own groups. They will almost always pick the same people to work with.

Each member of the group should have a specific role. First, assign Number 1s as group leaders (a great role for your most disruptive student). Their only job is to make sure everyone else is doing his or her job.

Once groups are seated and quiet (this is the leader's responsibility), give specific instructions for each member.

Number 2s could be the readers, Number 3s could be the note takers, Number 4s could be the writers, and Number 5s could be the group presenters. Of course, you can create any categories that fit your specific class or lesson, but be sure to change the roles around so students don't complain. Group leaders need to write down the instructions for all members. Other members only need to know what they must do.

It is always easier to extend than it is to take away. Figure out how much time the activity is going to take, then subtract five minutes from the total. For example, if we believe an activity will take 10 minutes, we tell the class it has to be done in five. By giving less time we create a sense of urgency, and there is a greater likelihood that kids will get right to work. If they are working well and five minutes passes, we can extend another few minutes.

It is not uncommon to hear students complain about not wanting to work with certain members of the group. To eliminate this complaining, simply say the following: "Class, I need to let you all know right now . . . some of you are going to complain this year about who you are working with during group time. I want to let you all know right now that if you complain about working with someone you will be with that person every day until you stop complaining." Now kids will think twice before complaining.

Bring groups back, but allow slower groups to finish

It is common to hear students say, "But we aren't finished yet." It is important that we extend the time if most groups are not finished. However, if it is just one or two slower groups, allow them to finish while beginning the next thing you are going to teach with everyone else. This way the students that are finished are not bored waiting for the other groups, and the slower groups aren't mad because they didn't have enough time. It is really the only way to please everyone within group dynamics.

Create a class book

One of the best ways to prevent disruption and aggression in the classroom is to have outstanding and creative lessons. Linda Steinberg, a fifth-grade veteran of 33 years, shared several helpful strategies to reduce unwanted behaviors and keep students engaged and enthused. She told us that problems often occurred in her classroom when children had too much time on their hands. Ms. Steinberg told us that one way to combat this problem was to have ongoing projects that could be worked on at any time.

One idea to build community and keep students engaged was to create class books on different topics or subjects. Each student was given a letter of the alphabet. The class then created an alphabet book for whatever they were working on. For example, Ms. Steinberg had her students create a book about the Southeastern United States after learning about the history, people, and geography of that region. The assignment was clearly mapped out so that students of all abilities could participate meaningfully. Each student was given a letter and was allowed to choose a state in the targeted region. They were then required to choose something meaningful and representative of the state that also emphasized the letter they were given. Students were encouraged to use as many different media as they wanted, including magazines, newspapers, books, and the Internet (addressing multiple learning styles) to learn about their state. Illustrations were encouraged but not required so that those students who were poor artists would stay engaged (providing choice).

For example, one student given the letter "A" picked the word "alligator" for Florida. In the center of the page he cut out a picture of an alligator. He then had to write at least one complete sentence about the picture on his page. The sentence could, but did not have to, begin with the letter "A" but the key word with the main letter (alligator, in this case) had to be used and underlined in all the sentences in which it was used (establishing expectations that could be met by all). For example, this student wrote, "<u>A</u>lligator <u>a</u>tt<u>a</u>cks in Florid<u>a</u> h<u>a</u>ve become more common over the p<u>a</u>st few ye<u>a</u>rs."

Naturally, all assignments need to be modified to meet your individual class and grade level. For example, if your class is working on a specific state, each student could select or be given a letter for a state book. There could be many applications of this project for review and synthesis of explorers, presidents, and important current or historical events. Most great lessons have specific, purposeful goals that incorporate multiple learning styles in which all students have a good chance for success.

Make your own trading cards

A fun and engaging way for students to integrate information about important people or places they are studying is to create trading cards. Cards must have the following characteristics:

The country the famous person comes from

Why the person is famous

How the person impacted society

The dates or era during which the person lived

Why it is important to know about the person

Take a look at the cards for the athlete Wilma Rudolph and General Ulysses S. Grant done by fifth- and eleventh-grade students:

Name: Wilma Rudolph

Dates: 1940–1994

Country: USA

Sport: Track and Field

Famous for: When she was born she had a bad leg. She had braces on her legs. When she was 9 she got them off. When she was 11 she was a basketball star. She ran 20 races in the Olympics.

Name: Ulysses S. Grant

Dates: 1822–1885

Country: United States

Famous for: Grant was the most important general for the union during the civil war. His leadership and guidance helped the North win the war which eventually led to the abolition of slavery in the United States.

These cards can be done in all younger grades and some high school content areas. Be sure to laminate them for longer use.

Require students to watch television with a purpose

Can you imagine having a teacher who required you to watch NFL football in the fall and NBA basketball in the winter? A teacher in Green Bay, Wisconsin, does exactly that. This teacher works with inner-city kids and could not get them to learn fractions and percentages out of the textbook. Since most of her students loved sports, she began requiring that they watch football and basketball for homework. The teacher created her version of fantasy football and basketball leagues in her tenth-grade class. Students had to draft a quarterback, running back, receiver, kicker, and a defense. They were then required to watch the game and come in on Monday morning with statistics for each player on their team. For example, students would convert a quarterback's completion rate into a fraction and then convert the fraction to a percentage. She did this for running backs (to find average yards per game), receivers (average number of catches per game), and kickers (total number of points scored and field goal attempts). When football season ended, basketball took over. Students were not graded on how well their fantasy team performed, but on how well they converted their fantasy statistics. Many of her students had football and basketball teams going at the same time during November and December, creating a frenzy of interest. This teacher was excited to share her kids' newfound interest in fractions and percentages.

Use the story box

Students can create an actual box (cube) out of construction paper with six sides lettered A through F. A story box is an outline that helps organize what they are reading. Many students get confused when reading a story or play that has a lengthy character list. They forget names, what those characters did, and how they were important to the overall story. Each side of the box can be a different reminder.

For example, Side A might have the copyright date, author, title, and publisher of the story. Side B might list the names of the main characters and one important fact about each. Side C could list definitions of words, theme, plot, setting, and characterization. Side D could give one example of each related to the story being read. High school teachers can require more detail for each side of the story box. On Side E, high school students could write a summary as they understand it. Side F could be for the student to write a review of the story. Because reviews are opinion, they offer opportunities to teach the difference between summary and critique. When all story boxes are complete, students can use their box to study for tests, quizzes, or to help them write papers. Again, you can adapt this idea to your own unique classroom. Each side of the box can be individually created to fit your students' needs.

This can be done for all subjects. For instance, a math teacher can use a math box when teaching a problem with many different steps. Each side of the box is a different step in the problem. It can be a great way to get kids to remember difficult formulas and equations without getting overwhelmed.

Use word games such as Scrabble

Some games, such as Scrabble, can be great teaching tools. In this game, players build words using seven letters in their hand. This is a good method for building vocabulary. The game can also be played to build math skills, because each letter has a point value giving each completed word a different score. The double- and triple-letter and double- and triple-word spaces require students to use basic multiplication and addition. The only caution is to guard against games getting too competitive. We don't want students focusing on winning, but on building their math and English skills. Students can keep a record of points achieved in each game so they can compare current performance against their past as a noncompetitive way to note progress. With younger kids or special education students, you can play the game without points. This way they can focus all their energy on word building.

Play chess with a purpose

Chess also has huge benefits in the classroom. According to Yaussi (2004), chess indirectly teaches kids how to make good and wise decisions in life. Student chess players admitted that instead of making impulsive decisions and saying impulsive things, they would stop and think. The game of chess requires players to think about their own moves and their opponent's moves many steps ahead. They must evaluate both sides of the board and make adjustments as needed. When teaching seventh grade, I (BDM) played chess with my students after class. One student always wanted to play, but he was so slow that I was afraid the game would be torture. We finally played and the game did take forever, but he won. I learned that slow doesn't mean incompetent. In schools where chess is played, reading scores increase (Yaussi, 2004). Students were so competitive that they began reading books on chess strategy. This helped build vocabulary and comprehension skills.

Last year I began playing chess with my eleventh-grade students who were disruptive and emotionally challenged. At first they were frustrated with the game and had a hard time understanding it. But the more they played, the better they became. Students began asking to stay after school so they could play chess. I noticed a sharp increase in their thinking and reasoning skills. It was also a good tool for me to point to when reminding them not to make impulsive or rash decisions that would hurt them later. I would tell them,

"Remember, sometimes in chess you have to give up a pawn in order to save the queen. Don't get in a fight because another kid calls you a name. Walking away is like giving up the pawn to save much aggravation down the line." The phrase, "save the queen" became quite popular around the classroom.

Be careful when using games

In many classrooms games are used as review tools for tests and quizzes. The most popular seems to be some form of the television game show *Jeopardy*.

I (BDM) was working in an inclusion social studies class with a first-year teacher, Kerry Halof. Ms. Halof is wonderful. She has an excellent personality and warm demeanor combined with firm but fair policies, which make her a joy to work with. To prepare for an upcoming test, she and I decided to review with the class by having the students play *Jeopardy*. Five categories with different point level questions from 200 to 1,000 ranging from easiest to most difficult were established. We then divided the class into two teams with the rule being that each student would get a chance to answer a question for a certain amount of points. Ms. Halof called on students and they decided on a point level question to answer. It started off well until a shy boy named Frank was called on. His voice cracking nervously, Frank asked for "Geography for 200." Ms. Halof read the question and within seconds it was evident that he did not know the answer. Others around him began raising their hands and Frank lowered his eyes and put his head down. Ms. Halof quickly realized that Frank felt terrible and allowed a teammate to help him answer. This was the best she could do at that moment. However, Ms. Halof and I made eye contact and knew we had to discuss this later.

Students like Frank can become overwhelmed with anxiety while playing highly competitive intellectual games. They may shut down and even be unable to pay attention to other students' answers. Hence, successful review is not really taking place. It takes a good deal of self-confidence to risk being wrong, because most students will avoid looking stupid at all costs. Furthermore, if competition is a prominent part of the game and the wrong answer costs the team a reward, harassment and insults may result (more on this in Chapter 8). Unfortunately, in places like the lunchroom and gym, other kids might say things like, "I can't believe you missed that. It was so easy," or, "How could you not know that answer? Everyone else knew it. You let us all down!" What a horrible way for a student to go through the rest of the day. It might not take much for a student to get physically ill, become more withdrawn, or become disruptive to protect his or her self-esteem.

It is important to carefully consider what we are trying to accomplish when playing games. Is review really happening? Does the game have solid academic value? Is there a high likelihood of someone being embarrassed or humiliated during the game? If so, think of an alternative to the game that can accomplish the same academic goal(s) without upsetting anyone in the class. Some teachers tell us that their students "love to play these games." We respond by saying, "Yes. And ours love ice cream and candy too. It doesn't make it good for them."

PART 3: STRATEGIES FOR ASSIGNING MATERIAL AND ASSESSING PERFORMANCE

Because academic achievement is the primary yardstick that many students use to measure their self-worth in school, educators must devise ways of helping each student become an academic winner. It is no surprise that the vast majority of students who cause trouble in school are among the academically unsuccessful. They often decide that there is much more honor in acting "bad" than in looking "stupid." Others just toss in the towel quietly while rage builds inside. We must use practices that prevent students from becoming discouraged learners, or use effective interventions when they are discouraged, so that a real sense of self-worth fueled by genuine accomplishment can build confidence.

The strategies in this section are designed to set students up for success.

Make personal improvement
the hallmark of success

Remember Abby? She was my (BDM's) student who wasn't going to do a "f***ing" thing this year. For the first two weeks she kept her promise! Then, unexpectedly, she amazed me by doing an assignment and in so doing provided an important lesson for all educators.

As a class, we were reading Shakespeare's *Hamlet*, in which the theme of deception is quite prominent. Having learned long ago that disaffected students are more likely to get engaged when the curriculum relates to their lives, I gave them an assignment to write about a time when they either deceived or were deceived by someone. The next day Abby handed me her paper. She said, "Mr. M, I did my assignment." Before I could respond Abby was gone.

I got home from work that night and began reading the papers. I read Ben's first. Ben had been in my class for the entire school year and his paper was very good. His thoughts went deep with impressive use of metaphor and contrast that made it quite enjoyable to read. After finishing Ben's, next on the pile was Abby's. It looked exactly like this:

There was a time in my life when I was deceived

It was by my boyfriend

We were at party

I was like Yo what's up with that other girl

He was like Yo I don't know

I was like Yo what do you mean you don't know

And he was like Yo, I told you I don't know

I was like Yo

And he was like Yo

I was like Yo

And he was like Yo

It was probably the worst paper I had ever seen in just about every way: no punctuation, no complete sentences, and few coherent thoughts. It was absolutely terrible! If Abby's paper was graded in comparison to Ben, there was little choice but to give an "F" or a generous "D." The likely result would be Abby again shutting down and doing no further work. She had already told me she hated my school, my class, and everything about me. If I failed her paper or gave it a low grade, my fear was that it would confirm everything she already believed about her ability to learn my subject. My job at this point was to change her perception of my class first. Then I could begin teaching her to write. My main goal was not this paper because the mere fact that she had turned something in was a huge step forward. The primary goal was to get her to do the next paper, and then the one after that! I gave her paper an "A." My reasoning was that Abby's paper was at least 100 percent better than the last paper she turned in. That seemed deserving of a good grade. Should her next assignment generate an A? Probably not. She would have to show improvement when compared to this paper. Certainly, I reasoned, there was at least now a decent chance of getting a next assignment. After giving back her paper, I was shocked at her reaction. She initiated the following conversation:

Abby: Mr. M, you think I'm stupid?

Mr. M: No. Why would you say that?

Abby: I've never gotten an A in English in my life and I know this ain't no A. I know an A when I see one and this ain't no A.

Mr. M: I can see why you think that, but you've lucked out. It is an A in my class. You see, I compare your work to your own previous work. And since this is the first assignment I've ever gotten from you, it is an A. Now don't get too excited because your next one might not be an A. Of course, if it is a huge improvement over this one, that will be an A too.

Abby: So Mr. M, a complete sentence, that's just a subject and a verb?

Mr. M.:   Yes.

Abby: So, "Abby runs." That's a sentence?

Mr. M.:   Yes.

Abby: I can do that.

Mr. M.:   I know. And by the way, when you are ready, a paragraph is only four or five of those sentences.

Abby: Really?

Mr. M.:   Sure. And the great thing about the English state test is that in each essay there are only four paragraphs.

Abby: Seriously?

Mr. M.:   Yes. And the whole test has four essays. How many paragraphs is that?

Abby: Only 16 paragraphs? That's all I have to write and I'll pass?

Mr. M.:   Not only pass, but you will do well!

Abby: I can do that.

Mr. M.:   I know. But we need to start with three good sentences. Then we'll move to the next step. And remember, if those sentences are much improved, there is a good chance your grade again will be an A!

Abby: Okay, Mr. M. I can do that.

If Abby failed that first assignment, this conversation probably never would have happened. Some behavior problems that lead to aggression occur because students fail early on and then give up. Abby worked hard that year, and got a 66 on the high-stakes state test, proving that it is the rare student who is hopeless. In four months she went from hating the class to passing the state exam. Too bad they don't have an honor roll for improvement, because Abby would have made it. She stopped disrupting and disturbing my class, and most important, she made herself and me proud by graduating from high school.

Value what is learned more than the grade

It is right and proper for educators to have high expectations of all students. Evaluation and feedback are important parts of this. Nobody benefits when mastery is made too easy. As a culture, we certainly need to know that our doctor, plumber, or airplane pilot has been properly trained and meets at least minimum standards of competence. Unfortunately for some, there is no perfect system of evaluation that acknowledges achievement while keeping hope alive. Therefore, as educators we often face difficult decisions in trying to make grades accurately reflect achievement while using them as a tool to inspire continued learning. My bias is to err on the side of the latter.

If we value grades and the rewards that come with them more than we value learning, it becomes very difficult for Abby to get an "A." After all, she begins to stand a chance to make honor roll if she keeps improving. Some might argue that not giving a grade but rather limiting feedback to comments for improvement about a paper at this level might be a better alternative. Perhaps. It can be challenging to care more about learning than about grading, though.

Although comparing students' work to their own previous work is a good practice for all students, the ones like Abby in particular stand a better chance of staying motivated when they are merely required to improve every day. Being better on Tuesday than they were on Monday is possible for any student in any grade in any class. . . .

Offer genuine positive comments about performance

Finding something positive to write can be difficult, as seen from Abby's essay. In her case, I wrote, "Great job getting this in" because, based on her history, I was truly proud that she made an effort. Those five words can be written on any paper. If we have it, then it was a great job getting it in. However, be careful not to overuse this phrase. It is best to find something concrete and specific that the student did well in addition to just handing it in.

Related to the assignment, I noticed that she had capitalized the first word of each sentence fragment. This let me know that she at least knew that the beginning of a sentence needed to be capitalized. I offered the following feedback: "Abby, great job getting this in. Now we need to work on punctuation." Trying to correct too much too soon often overwhelms students, leading to frustration and resignation. Here are several sample comments to use or modify when grading:

Thanks for the effort.

I thought your first example was really well done, even though you didn't get a chance to do the other three!

This was a tough assignment and I appreciate the effort you put in!

Even though it is not complete, I noticed your hard work and I appreciate your effort!

I totally see why you thought that way, and that is a very common mistake. In fact, I think I made that same mistake when I was in eighth grade!

I know you punched a locker and I'm not happy about it, but that is better than punching another person's face. We'll fix the locker tomorrow.

The progress I've seen from you is amazing. Keep working hard.

Collect homework at the end of class, and review it at the beginning

An extremely gifted English teacher, Jack Desan, shared the practice of going over homework at the beginning of class but collecting it at the end. Many educators might question this method because it is a good bet students that did not do the work will copy it in. Mr. Desan acknowledges that this happens often and makes the point that it is exactly what he wants to happen. His reasoning is that for some of these kids it is the only time they get the work done and "they have to take our exam too."

Many of these students will then hand in their notes or homework at the end of class and try to pass it off as if they completed the assignment on time. However, Mr. Desan quickly lets them know that he saw them copying in the work and then grades them accordingly. He also tells these students he hopes they will attempt their homework legitimately in the future. Some teachers spend valuable minutes at the beginning of class checking each student's work to see if it is complete. This is often a time where disruptive behavior occurs. Students who did not complete the work know they will soon be caught. They know being called on it is only moments away. This leads many of them to distract the teacher by misbehaving.

Ensure success by giving choices

Use choice in the classroom to motivate and ensure success. We recently met a math teacher who assigns 20 math problems to her class and requires them to choose the five easiest problems on the page. It generally does not take 20 problems for her to know if a student understands the material. It certainly does not take 20 problems to know a student does not understand the material. By asking for the five easiest, the students have to look at them all. Some will even do them all and then tell you which were the five easiest.

I (ANM) once tried this in my room and had a student tell me he didn't know the easiest, but that numbers 5, 8, and 10 were definitely the hardest. I asked why and she said it was because they were word problems and there was no way to muddle through all those words. Her response instantly told me that reading was the problem, not math. I started assigning fewer word problems and we worked more intensively on reading.

Other teachers allow students to do test corrections to raise their grade. We especially like the idea of giving students two or three chances to raise their grade if they are dissatisfied. For example, allowing students to retake a different form of the same test, if they choose, can be a good strategy to motivate reluctant test takers. Many study much harder to "learn from their mistakes" when they have the incentive of possibly doing better on the retake.

A teacher in New Mexico gives her class a wild card question on every quiz and test. Students can pick one question that they do not want to answer. In its place, they have to write another question that relates to the topic and answer it correctly. This gives them at least one answer guaranteed to be correct on the exam. Another teacher uses the same technique, but for a homework assignment. Students may trade any question for one they create and answer.

When I (RLC) recently visited a high school math class, one student gave a wrong answer. I watched with curiosity as the teacher worked with the student for several minutes until the student understood how to do the problem correctly while the rest of the class was getting started on homework. This teacher then gave her a full page of problems just like the ones she got wrong. He asked the girl to please complete any three on the page for homework. Later, I asked the teacher why he only wanted her to complete three. He told me that it would take her long enough just to do one problem. If he assigned all 20 she would surely give up. He told me, "While I can't always know exactly what to give each student, I certainly can do my best. And this kid could not do more than three problems. There is no way!"

Another colleague uses what she fondly calls her blue light special. About once a month students walk into class and find a blue light flashing, the kind you might see at Kmart to indicate a special sale. When this happens, students have one full period to complete any makeup work without penalty. Those without makeup work are encouraged to help their classmates for their own extra credit.

Highlight effort and praise mistakes

I (ANM) recently observed a self-contained class of low achievers who had gained a negative reputation among teachers in the school. As I watched these children I was struck by their obvious need to show that they didn't care about school. Many came unprepared, several collected zeroes, and several were quick to challenge authority. Yet they behaved differently with Ms. Jackson, their social studies teacher. She made each of her students actually feel good about making mistakes. As she returned an assignment to a student who received 60 percent, she said, "You did a great job on questions, 1, 6, 7, 8, 9, and 10. But I noticed that you didn't do the others. Those have to do with China and communism. I must not have done a very good job teaching that. I'll be reviewing that topic in the first few minutes of today's class. If you'd like to improve your grade, please redo those questions when I'm finished. Either way, congratulations on the answers you completed. They were done very well!" In her class, the students with behavior difficulties were highly motivated, concerned about their performance, and eager to improve. They loved Ms. Jackson and rarely disrupted her class.

Educators also need to highlight their own effort for a job well done even if it falls short of somebody else's standards. It is so important to make effort and improvement at least as much of a gold standard as outcome when measuring success. I (RLC) recently worked with a dejected teacher who tried hard to motivate three eleventh graders who had very challenging behavior issues. At the end of the year these students received scores of 46, 57, and 62 on their state assessment. The teacher was bummed about the kids not passing (the passing score was 65) and upset that the state and her administration might view her year as unsuccessful. She explained that the year before, on a similar exam, these same students had scores of 22, 27, and 31. It is sad that students can improve 100 percent from one year to the next, but the teacher responsible feels like a failure. If any of us grew our money in the stock market by 100 percent in a year, would we consider the strategy a failure?

Since effort and improvement are not rewarded in most places, the scores are still viewed as failures. Administrators should reward improvements, even if the final score does not meet the standards.

A fourth-grade teacher, Becky Zelesnikar from Greece, New York, told us how she rewarded mistakes in her classroom to encourage risk taking by her students. Each day she had a "Mistake of the Day." From the previous night's homework Ms. Zelesnikar picked one mistake that she believed was so good it could be made by anyone. The student was privately told of the mistake and then asked if it could go on the board as the Mistake of the Day. She then reviewed the homework by using this mistake as an example of a very smart, intelligent person, making a very good mistake. She told us that this encouraged others to admit their mistakes. Ms. Zelesnikar also told us there was a carryover to all aspects of school. She said her students were more apt to admit a problem on the playground or in the lunchroom because they learned that no one is perfect and that they all make mistakes.

It takes a love of learning to genuinely rejoice in the mistakes of our students. We know another teacher who regularly thanks her students for making errors that others can learn from. For example, it is not unusual for her to say, "Tanika made an excellent mistake. She did the whole long division problem correctly except she added instead of subtracted. That serves as a good reminder of how to do something well, but not paying attention to those little things like plus and minus signs can make a big difference. Thanks for making that mistake Tanika. We can all learn from it."

Focus on the positive, especially when it's hard to find

Some students are hard to appreciate. They irritate us and know exactly what buttons to press and how to press them for maximum irritation. It is easy to understand the desire to withdraw or to fight with such students. Yet we must remember that their angry, negative ways often reflect their own self-hatred and misguided life events, not ours. Although interacting with these students can be unappealing, it is our professional responsibility to continue looking for ways to turn them around. Wise teachers invest preventive time by regularly calling or writing students and their parents at home to share appreciations, ask for suggestions, and provide feedback.

Another teacher, John Stevens, described Jenny as an attention-seeking, disruptive girl who yawned loudly in class. Sweet smiles and insincere apologies usually followed. Mr. Stevens decided to write Jenny's parents a note. He told them how much he enjoyed having her in class and that she was a bright student with a delightful sense of humor and a B average. She handed the note to Jenny, unsealed, and asked that it be given to her parents.

Mr. Evans was a high school biololgy teacher in Fairfax, Virginia. He tried hard to get Russell to class on time. He talked with him, called his home, gave late slips and detention, and kicked him out of class. Frustrated by Russell's continued tardiness, Mr. Evans used a "paradoxical" method, which is a way of changing behavior by encouraging its very continuation. Such methods are designed to appreciate the very behavior we want to put to an end by emotionally removing ourselves from power struggles. These methods require an attitude that the student is more important than the behavior. In this case, Mr. Evans approached Russell after class and said, "Russell, I would like you to be in class on time, but for reasons I don't understand, it's just not happening. Even though I am not happy that you come late, you are an important member of our class. I can see that you listen, sometimes give an answer, and are quite friendly to others. If there is anything I can do to help get you here earlier, please let me know. If not, I'd rather see you late than not at all."

Growing numbers of students who lack adequate nurturing and attention will resist change when they don't trust. Because people are often frightened by change, they are more apt to take a risk when not forced to let go of the familiar. In the presence of an encouraging teacher who invites but does not demand change, many youth will try an alternative behavior because they will be accepted either way. In Russell's case, change was not possible because, as the oldest of several children in a single-parent family, he was responsible for seeing the younger children off to school. While Russell continued to come late, Mr. Evans reported a marked improvement in his attitude after their talk.

KEY POINTS FROM THE CHAPTER

It takes effort to work at building relationships with students with behavior difficulties. A strong relationship is an important ingredient when influencing behavior change. Although teaching great lessons may seem unrelated to student disruption and aggression, there is a direct correlation. When students feel hopeful that reasonable effort can lead to success, they are usually more motivated to achieve and less likely to disrupt.

Sometimes we need to pick the best of bad options. We would rather a student do nothing in class than nothing somewhere else in the building. Remember, it is okay and important to compare and grade student work compared to their previous work so improvement becomes at least one standard for success.

Do not let others influence your feelings about a student. Remember to care more about learning than about grading and you will succeed with just about any "Abby" in your class.

Be sure to give students real legitimate choices and then allow them to live with the consequences of those choices.

Highlight and reward effort at least as much and as often as outcomes.

6

Developing Effective Rules

S tudents need secure, confident, respectful adults that are
appropriately firm and demanding when they cross the
line. In some of our earlier books, we wrote about the importance of having clear and specific rules connected to a set of
principles or values that define the classroom atmosphere
(Curwin & Mendler, 1998). Readers who want specific step-
by-step guidelines in establishing school or classroom rules
are referred to these earlier works. Here, we will focus on how
educators can interact with students so that the implementa-
tion of rules is most effective. Our observations lead us to
believe that how we do things is as important as what we do.
The goal of all schools and teachers should be good rules that
are effectively enforced.

Administrators should attempt to create policies that provide for the safety of students. Within the classroom, each
teacher should emphatically support principles of nonvio-
lence, have rules that support these principles, and then teach
appropriate alternatives for expressing anger and frustration.

The most effective and respected teachers express their
beliefs, demands, and expectations within the context of clear
values and goals. They have found a way to be firm and hold

students accountable while treating them with dignity and maintaining their own dignity.

Many teachers have impulsive students whose behavior can quickly escalate to hostility. We must learn and remind ourselves how to enforce rules without resorting to threats, while doing our best to be assertive and respectful. We must try hard to stay in control of ourselves at all times.

Take a few moments to reflect on specific rules that you think are necessary for good learning and teaching to occur. Identify the value or principle that guides the rule. Discipline is best when students know what to do (rules) and why it is necessary (values and principles).

Concepts such as respect, responsibility, and safety are not rules, they are values. Educators develop specific rules to promote the values needed for good learning and teaching to occur. Rules are specific, concrete, and leave no room for interpretation.

One example is the way airlines separate rules and values. The value of all airlines is safety. The flight attendant identifies this value, then specifies the rules: at take-off, seat belts must be fastened; seat backs and tray tables must in their full, upright position; and all electronic devices must be turned off. Notice that values are based on attitude, rules are based on behavior. Schools work best when they follow the same pattern. Some examples follow.

Value: We expect to have a safe school.
Rule: keep your hands and feet to yourself.

Value: Put forth your best effort when doing your work.
Rule: Hand in work within 24 hours of it being assigned.

Value: There is more than one opinion about most things and tolerance is necessary, even when you disagree with somebody.
Rule: Settle disagreements with words, not fists.

Use this process when developing values and rules

The two values all schools can begin with are (1) Everybody has the right to be and feel safe, and (2) All who enter here will learn. To further develop values and rules, the following questions can be used as a guide:

1. What values do you find important in the classroom? Be specific.

2. How can you encourage students to create rules based on these values?

3. How do these rules support learning and safety? Imagine your students are in front of you. Tell them how you think their learning will improve and their safety will increase by following these rules.

4. Is the rule current? If a rule is outdated do not be afraid to change or get rid of it. We are all more likely to follow rules that make sense.

Encourage meaningful student involvement

Disruptive students often feel powerless, but there are ways of signaling and demonstrating that they have influence over what happens to them, and that their input at school is valued and important. In the "Discipline With Dignity" program (Curwin & Mendler, 1998), we advocate that schools involve students as decision makers and problem solvers. They can be invited to assist in developing values, principles, rules, and consequences in the classroom. When problems occur, student input can be helpful. It gives them a sense of involvement and ownership that often translates into commitment and responsibility. It is not unusual for some of the youngsters with the most difficult behaviors to become class behavior monitors when empowered in this way. They begin to monitor each other and, eventually, themselves.

When students' thoughts and opinions are valued and are important enough to influence policy, they are participating in a democratic decision-making process. Making decisions while realizing that some will be supported and others will not be is an essential life skill for success in our culture.

A growing number of students have little actual control in their lives. Students need us to help them feel in control. Listening to their thoughts and giving them a voice in routines, activities, and rules affecting them can make a positive difference. The most effective way to get kids to follow the rules of a school or classroom is to let them have a say in what those rules are. Educators often think that a good discipline policy means we make rules and kids follow them. The problem is that all people have a basic need to sense that they are in control or have some power. One suggestion is that you take two to four of your students with the most difficult behaviors from each grade level (depending on school size) and create a "rules committee." The committee will also include the principal, assistant principal, head security person, at least two teachers, and possibly two to four parents. You can adjust your faculty involvement based on what you think your school needs.

The committee can meet before the school year begins and develop a rules plan that the students and faculty will follow. At your meetings, it is helpful to sit at an oval or round table so all people can see each other and feel like equals. At the first meeting, the principal explains how important this committee is to the safety and effectiveness of the school. Each member is asked to write down what he or she believes are the most important components of a safe school. At this point, the components of a safe school should not be seen as rules. Rather, the faculty leader explains to the students that these are more important than rules. They are the values that we must live by in school and in society. It is helpful to explain to the committee that values should be broad and general.

An example of these broad values is, "We will respect this place, each other, and ourselves." If used as part of a rule, the word "respect" can be confusing. For example, in Mr. Jones's class, wearing a hat is allowed. He even has a contest once a year to see who can wear the funkiest hat. However, in the same school Ms. Alhart thinks hats are disrespectful and does not allow them. Therefore, if Mr. Jones and Ms. Alhart have "be respectful" posted only as a rule, students must figure out what that word means to each teacher.

After a value such as "safety" is agreed on, it is time to formulate rules for that value. Students create a rule for themselves, as do teachers. For example, your students might agree that hitting is unsafe. Therefore the rule will say, "Keep hands, feet, and other body parts to yourself at all times." Remember, it is easier to enforce rules that students help create.

At the initial rules committee meeting, the principal will give the students and staff no more than 15 minutes to come up with values. After each group has ranked them from most to least important, the students select a student representative to present the ones they have chosen. It is a good idea to ask them to explain why they came up with these selections. The teachers then do the same. After both groups have listed their values, compare both lists. Many of the same values probably will appear on both lists. The next step is for all members of the committee to agree on the most important values. These will be the foundation of the school for that year. The principal can make it clear that these values might change during the year, based on recommendations of the committee and changing school needs. Make sure that students and faculty are aware that values will be observed by everyone in the school, and not just by students.

When this step is complete, each committee member writes down one specific rule that relates directly to the value. For example, if "responsibility" is a value, a rule for students might be, "All students must bring a writing utensil and paper to class every day." A rule for teachers might be, "All papers will be graded and handed back within two days of being submitted." After each committee member has written a rule based on the value, have each present the rule to the group. The committee discusses which rules (if any) based on the values should be followed by everyone.

Students are more likely to agree to rules for themselves when they know teachers and administrators have to follow rules as well. Once values and rules are agreed on, the committee posts the values in the front of the building for all to see. The posting needs to articulate that these are the values that are at the core of school policy. It should also make clear the rules that the committee agreed all members of the school community should follow. Each teacher then leads his or her class in a discussion of rules and values.

We also like the idea of substituting the word "expectation" for the word "rule" because kids with tough behaviors are known for their willingness to break rules. They have a harder time not meeting expectations.

Finally, it is helpful for this committee to meet regularly (at first once every two weeks) for an update on how things are going. This gives the principal a chance to meet with students and faculty in a productive way so that all feel as if they are a part of something crucial to the success of the school. It is particularly important that the student members of the committee are viewed as the voice of their classmates. Allow them to bring concerns, thoughts, feelings, and ideas to the attention of school staff. If a rule is not working, it is crucial to the success of the school that it be modified.

These are the benefits of student involvement in developing rules

While I (BDM) was teaching in a small school district with about 550 students in Grades 7 to 12, the principal believed that students were just visitors, and that they should follow the rules that the administration made. In fact, he did not believe in allowing even teachers to have much say about what the rules were. The year was spent battling with kids about rules they did not think were necessary.

One rule that was especially disturbing was the hat rule. Countless hours were spent asking kids to take their hats off in the hall. Some of us would bet on how many minutes it would take at faculty meetings before the principal would bring up kids and hats. One day I was attempting to enforce this rule. I asked one of my students to please take his hat off. He responded by saying, "Why? What's the point of the rule?" Not having a great answer, I simply said, "Sometimes we have to follow rules in life that we don't like. When you get out of school you will have to follow the rules of society even if you don't like them." At that moment, another student offered, "That is only partially true. In society if we don't like a rule or a law we have the power to try to change that rule. And people break rules and laws all the time and get away with them as long as they aren't hurting others."

"Explain," I said.

He continued, "Are you telling us that you don't ever break rules? I'll bet that you don't always follow the speed limit! Aren't you more likely to follow the speed limit when there are cars all around you rather than when the road is empty? Aren't you more likely to slow down on a residential street when children are playing than late at night? You might have been speeding but you weren't being irresponsible on the road. So stop telling us that you have to enforce these rules because it is for our own good. That's nonsense. We follow rules that make sense, just like you do."

I could not argue with his logic. When he was finished I said, "That's a great point and I really appreciate you sharing. But until a law is changed you can still get a ticket even if nobody is around while you are speeding. So thanks for taking your hat off." He smiled, and removed his hat.

There was not a rules committee at this school, but revisiting this rule would have been a good idea if there had been. Adults show great wisdom when they change rules that make little sense. Eliminating those rules that make little sense will strengthen those that make the most sense. A rules committee in this school might have agreed that Friday would be hat day, but Monday through Thursday no hats allowed. If students agreed to this, it would become easier to enforce the rules during the week. Instead of saying "take the hat off," we could say, "It was your idea to have hat day on Friday. Isn't today Wednesday?"

Here are a few guidelines to follow with students and rules:

1. Allow students to create rules. The classroom rules cannot violate a schoolwide rule or a law, and the rule cannot interfere with the learning process.

2. Ask for student input in as many areas of the classroom as possible.

3. The majority of the class must agree for the rule to be implemented.

4. Ask for student input when devising consequences for misbehavior. Allow students to make mistakes, and allow them to live with the consequences of those mistakes.

5. Be firm but flexible as long as safety and learning will not suffer. For example, if students propose "no homework," the teacher may agree to no homework one night per week, but not five. She or he can then allow students to decide or vote on which will be "no homework" night.

Encourage class problem solving when rules are broken

When problems persist with one or more students, there is little doubt that all others in the class are negatively affected. While the educator is the classroom leader, he or she is not the only one responsible for defining and maintaining standards. Students can be helpful by using their collective powers of persuasion on those who interfere with the learning process. This is most effective when the student leaders are on our side. The strategy below can be used with the entire class or just with those students who seem to exert the greatest influence on their peers. When safety is the issue, students need either assurance or reassurance that their teacher will be the primary person in the classroom who will handle the situation. But students also can be involved as partners in solving problems when they occur. This is an excellent way to teach kids responsibility. Establishing basic problem-solving procedures and then using them can be very effective. We suggest the following:

1. Ask students what is *good* about the problem. This requires them to define the problem clearly. For example, "What is good about calling people names?

What is good about being called a name?" We begin with asking what is good about a problem because it helps students see the benefits derived from the situation. Problems rarely are solved until people realize and understand what sustains the problem behavior.

2. Ask students what is *bad* about the problem. This gives them a chance to express how their learning and perhaps safety is threatened by the problem or the problem student. For example, "What is bad about calling people names? What is bad about being called a name?"

3. List all possible solutions to the problem. Use basic brainstorming procedures, and then list all possible solutions. These may cover suggestions for the teacher to solve the problem, suggestions for students to help solve the problem, suggestions for the problem student to solve the problem, or suggestions for others in school or outside to help solve the problem.

4. Decide on the best possible solution to the problem. After deciding on the best possible solution, work with the student, other teachers, administrators, and possibly parents on implementing what you came up with.

KEY POINTS FROM THE CHAPTER

Be sure rules are specific and make sense.

Remember that values and rules are different. Confusing them will often cause behavior problems.

Do not be afraid to get rid of a rule that is outdated. This will help strengthen those that are still relevant.

Allow students to have a say in helping create, develop, and implement rules.

Be sure to have rules for the teacher as well as the students.

7

Handling Power Struggles Effectively

Power struggles happen in a classroom because the teacher and student both want the same thing. The student does not want to look bad in front of the teacher and the teacher does not want to look bad in front of the class. So the argument begins. It might go something like this:

Teacher: (standing) Do it now.

Student: (sitting) No. I don't want to.

Teacher: Yes.

Student: No.

Teacher: Yes.

Student: No.

This goes back and forth until finally the teacher has the last word. Usually the last word is some variation of, "GET OUT OF MY CLASSROOM!"

Student: (*now visibly agitated, perhaps flipping the chair over*)
Man, this class is stupid anyway. You think I care?
I don't care. I'll leave. Mr. Principal likes me better
than you anyway. He'll listen to me. You're a bitch.

If we are lucky, the student then slams the door open and
leaves. If we are not lucky, the student stays. Many younger
kids are scared and do not want to leave. So they stay, often
running away as the teacher attempts to get them to leave.
Other students find this amusing or scary (neither of which is
good for the learning environment) and the class becomes a
chaotic mess. And, of course, kids who leave the classroom
never go directly to the principal's office. They go meet up with
the other kids who have been kicked out of other classes. They
walk by the cafeteria and the gym and sometimes even the
very classroom they were just kicked out of! Eventually they
strut into the principal's office looking completely calm. They
say good morning to the secretary, and regulars go directly to
their chairs and wait patiently. The principal opens the office
door, the student walks in, and the following conversation
takes place in every school office across this great country.

Principal: What did you do this time?

Student: Nothing.

Principal: Well, then why are you here?

Student: I don't know.

Good administrators are able to get some kids to take a
little bit of responsibility.

Principal: So you did absolutely nothing? I find that hard to
believe.

Student: Well, I might have called her a bitch. But she is
one! Can you believe the way she talks to kids?
She is so rude, and she smells like a mixture of cof-
fee and cigarettes! Tell her to mix in some gum!
And my brother had her last year and he said the
same thing then, and my mom had her 25 years

ago and she was mean then too. Can you believe that old bag is still teaching? Dang, can't you find someone younger?

Meanwhile, teachers are no better. Do you really think the principal is going to wave a magic wand and the kid will get better? Whose side does the administrator always hear first? The student's. By the time the administrator gets the referral from the teacher the incident has usually been dealt with. And what does every teacher in this great country write on every referral form? That the student was insubordinate, disrespectful, rude, or inappropriate. If the referral is handwritten, we can sense the teacher's anger by the way the letters are carved into the form. Instead of doing that, write the truth: "One of us had to leave and I figured I'd get in trouble if it was me, so I sent the student!"

When these battles occur in a school, it is serious business. Eventually the student comes back to class, unscathed, usually looking happier than ever. And now teachers, instead of being mad at the kid, are mad at the administrator. Students who make trouble are very good at getting teachers and administrators to hate each other. Often they succeed, which is why we take you all the way back to the initial yes/no conversation. The following is a step-by-step process for defusing disruptive behavior.

Step 1. Recognize the conflict and point out what is at stake. Remember that we are adults and they are kids. We are highly trained professionals and they are *kids*. If we can learn to see the argument coming and point it out before the escalation occurs, usually the conflict ends.

Teacher: Please do problems 1 to 10.

Student: No. I don't want to do 10 problems.

Teacher: If we keep going like this, an argument could break out. I don't want to look bad in front of the group and I know you don't, either. I'd prefer you do what I ask, but I'm happy to discuss this with you after class. At that time you can try to convince me why 10 problems are too many. Thanks for waiting until then.

Then get out of there. Get back to teaching. If we stick around and wait for a response, nothing good is going to happen. We are not interested in hearing from the student right then. After class we will discuss it if the student still remembers what the argument was about!

Step 2. Ignore the hook, and become a second-to-last-word person. We mentioned earlier that students are great at hooking us back into conflicts. When we point out what is at stake and move our lesson forward, students almost always mumble something under their breath. Train your ear to ignore the hook. Teaching is a predictable business. In the early stages of a power struggle, ignoring is usually the best way. Many teachers believe that by not having the last word they look weak in front of their class. In fact, the opposite is true. We stay strong by moving our lesson forward.

Andy Skillings, a science teacher in Rochester, Minnesota, understood this concept very well. Every time a student called him a name under his breath he would write the name down in his "notebook of insults." Each night he would review with his wife the names he had to endure in order to stay out of power conflicts with kids. "My wife couldn't wait to get home so she could hear some names my students called me." She would then agree or disagree (the latter a bit more often) with the student's assessment of her husband. At the end of each school year, Mr. Skillings gave out a best insult award to a student that his wife thought was most deserving. We are not here to judge whether or not we would use the exact same approach, but if the goal is truly to defuse, he was right on the money. He was ignoring the hook, and then having some fun with it.

Step 3. Model the values and behaviors you want to see. Students learn morals and actions based on what they see more than what they hear. Morals are constantly developing. It is never too late to become a morally strong person. It is not easy to respond to kids the way we want them to respond to us. Below are some specific examples of how to encourage them to respond appropriately.

Teacher:	Chris, I'd prefer you didn't talk to me that way. Is there something bothering you?
Chris:	F**k you.
Teacher:	I'll take that as a "no," even though we both know there is a more respectful way to say it. *(Then walk away.)*

We often hear teachers tell their students to "just walk away" when someone calls them a name or says something they don't like. Teachers tell students all the time, if someone is bothering you just ignore them. If someone says something you don't like, turn and walk the other way. Remember, students are much more likely to walk away when they see their teacher model this behavior in a similar circumstance. It is much easier said than done.

Step 4. Use the PEP technique (Mendler, 1997). PEP is the acronym for privacy, eye contact, and proximity. It is best used during the early stages of student behavior that is annoying to you. For example, Andrea and Erica are in the back, disrupting class. During the normal course of the lesson, the teacher wanders toward them, without stopping the lesson. The teacher then stops at Andrea's desk, quickly gets down to her level (*proximity*), makes strong *eye contact*, and tells her as quietly (*privacy*) and firmly as possible, "Cut it out." It is so important for the teacher to then get out of there and continue teaching. A few seconds later the next stop is at Matt's (a different student in the class) desk to use PEP again. This time the teacher stops by and tells him, "Great job on your homework last night. I'm really proud of you." Again, the teacher gets out of there and continues teaching. This is not a time to stick around for a response from either one of the students. Sticking around after delivering a PEP message invites a response and is the Number 1 reason the technique fails. Occasionally Andrea will respond anyway. Usually it will be something like, "Cut what out? I wasn't doing anything." This is a great time to look at the student, shake your head, and continue teaching. Remember, when PEP is used properly it is done so quickly and so privately that the rest of the class does not see it happen. Now Andrea risks looking foolish for blurting, "Cut what out?" in front of the entire class.

Remember, PEP does not work if teachers are always delivering negative messages. Students quickly figure out that every time you stop by it is to correct them. Their guard goes up, and the strategy becomes ineffective. However, if you stop by their desks just as often to deliver a positive or neutral message, you become less predictable, the student's guard doesn't go up, and both messages can be effective.

Some students will wonder what you said to the person receiving the PEP message. Telling the entire class early in the year something like, "I will be delivering private messages to individual students during the year. Those messages are intended only for that person. I will not share those messages with everyone. Understand that I will be delivering messages to you just as often as to your friends. The messages will be used to tell you things that I like and that you are doing well, and things I don't like and think you need to improve on."

Of course some students will forget and wonder, "What did he say?" Now we don't have to stop our lesson to respond because another student will remind them that the message was not for everyone's ears. If no one remembers, we simply remind them that the messages are for individual ears only.

Step 5. Be careful using sarcasm. If used incorrectly, sarcasm can leave a victim behind. Rhetorical questions are a great example of this and we hear teachers use them all the time. Rhetorical questions are usually nasty. They are often said out loud with the primary intention to embarrass the student. I (RLC) learned to stop using these during my first year working with a mildly autistic student, Nathan. He always told the truth, and took everything I said literally. One conversation went like this:

Mr. C.:   Nathan, how many times do I have to tell you to bring your pencil?

Nathan: Twenty-six so far and I'm still forgetting. Sorry. I'm thinking it will take about 50 *(said with a serious demeanor)*. Usually that's how many times people have to tell me things that don't interest me before I remember or respond. Bringing my pencil doesn't interest me. My parents say that it should, but it doesn't. I can't make things interest me that don't. This really makes my mom and dad mad because they get like you and get really upset with me sometimes. Then they say I'm being a "smart ass" but I'm not really sure what being a "smart ass" is. I've asked before, but this makes them even madder. They've learned that if I care about something, you only have to tell me once, and then I remember. So based on my calculations, probably just about 24 more times and then I'll remember.

Imagine if all students answered rhetorical questions this way? Teachers would stop asking them. Teach your nonautistic students to respond in the same sort of way.

Teacher: What am I gonna do with you?

Student: I'll take two tickets to the World Series, please.

Unfortunately, most students are not witty enough to answer this way. When they do, the teacher responds with another rhetorical question or sarcastic remark that ultimately ends in an argument or power struggle. Kids often become embarrassed and ashamed. Their misery and anger then continue to grow. When teachers use sarcastic language they often forget about the comment a few minutes later. Students don't forget so quickly. Many will hold on to the remark and replay it over and over in their mind. They wonder if we were serious and begin getting defensive when we talk to them. Remember, sarcasm works only when the person knows we are being sarcastic. That's the whole point of it!

Step 6. Listen, acknowledge, agree, defer (LAAD). There are four important keys in the defusing process. (This works not just with students, but with everyone.)

Listen: Hear what students are saying, not how they are saying it.

Acknowledge: Let students know in a firm but noncritical way that you hear them.

Agree: Let students know that what they are saying is or might be true.

Defer: Let students know you will discuss this at a later time.

These skills can be very useful in many situations beyond school. When asked what went wrong with their marriage in an informal survey of recently divorced couples, 86 percent of them had at least one member (and more than 50 percent had both members) say they felt their partner didn't listen. More than 70 percent of the couples said their partner didn't acknowledge their needs, and if they had, they might have felt differently. Nearly 92 percent of the couples felt that their partner almost never admitted when he or she was wrong. When asked about discussing their feelings at a later time, most said they did not defer because the first three steps were not taken. Most claimed that they would have been much more likely to discuss the issues during a calmer moment.

Imagine you teach high school math and a new principal with a math background is hired. He decides that he is going to revamp the math department for next year. Wondering what this means, you call the principal and the following conversation takes place:

Teacher: I'm wondering if I can give you my thoughts on revamping the math department. I have some good suggestions for how to make it better.

Principal: Thanks for the offer, but I'm really busy this summer. I'm not sure if you've heard, but I have a math background. I know how a good math department should be run, and that is what I am going to do. And besides, I'm the principal here now. I will make the decision based on what I feel is best. See you in September.

How would this make you feel? Would you have any interest in working for your new boss? Would you think he or she was arrogant? Now, instead of that conversation, imagine that this one occurs:

Teacher: I'm wondering if I can give you my thoughts on revamping the math department.

Principal: Sure. I'd love to hear them. Please understand, I'm not promising I will do what you think, but I will certainly consider it when finishing the revamping. Sound good?

Teacher: Sure. I think . . .

Principal: (after listening) Thanks so much for the suggestions. Some of them are really excellent and I will take them into consideration. I hope you will not be too upset if not all of your suggestions are incorporated, but thanks so much for sharing them. My door is always open for thoughts and suggestions from my staff.

The second example was very different from the first. By taking a few minutes to listen ("Sure, you can tell me what you think"), acknowledge ("Thanks for sharing"), agree ("Your ideas are good"), and defer ("You can always come and see me"), this administrator is viewed in a positive way. Finally, imagine that the second conversation happened, then you came back from summer vacation to find that none of your ideas had been implemented (worst case scenario). Wouldn't you still feel good about the fact that you were consulted before the decisions were made? Even though your ideas were not implemented, you had a say and know the door is open for you to continue having a say.

We hope you see the analogy with students. Allow them to have their say, even if your mind is already made up about something. (Try to keep a little slit open, though.) Let them think you value their opinion (even if you don't agree with them) and you will strongly consider it when making your final decision. If you do this, students are much more likely to live with the decision that is made.

Step 7. Use humor. Some teachers are great at doing impersonations of movie characters or music stars. Responding in the voice of a famous person (even if it is not done well) will startle the student who is misbehaving, and often will get the student back on task.

A final story of using humor to defuse happened in Brighton, Colorado. A social studies teacher was in the middle of asking for homework when a student jumped up and said, "I don't have it, you giraffe-looking motherf***er." The teacher backed away from the student and looked at his class. He said to them, "Do I look like a giraffe?" To which a different student responded, "Well Mr. Hanley, you do have a long neck and a big nose. You do sort of look like a giraffe." The class laughed, Mr. Hanley smiled as well, and continued with his lesson. He spoke with the inappropriate student after class about her behavior.

When faced with inappropriate student behavior, keep in mind your two main goals: keep your students in class and get back to teaching.

KEY POINTS FROM THE CHAPTER

Power struggles almost never happen in private, which means the other students play a role. Students always need to look good in front of each other. It is okay for the teacher to back down, and defer to a later time. Remember to point out what's at stake to the student: "You and I are about to argue right now. You don't want to look bad in front of the class and neither do I, so let's talk about it later. Thanks." Then move on. Get out of there. Continue teaching.

Use PEP whenever possible, and don't forget to listen, acknowledge, agree, and defer. Finally, it is okay to laugh at yourself once in a while. This goes a long way in defusing most situations.

8

Strategies for Teaching Students to Handle Conflict Effectively

Although bullying and other forms of aggression are often identified as major issues in our schools, few educators spend sufficient time teaching students more effective ways to manage their frustration and anger. Most of us are so focused on covering curriculum that we don't take time to educate students on what they can do or say when someone picks on them or says something they don't like. This chapter provides suggestions and strategies that teachers can share to help students deal constructively with frustration and anger so they do not get into trouble by escalating a problematic situation into aggressive words or deeds.

Preventing harmful aggression means more than just responding to a situation when it happens. Students need practical problem-solving strategies that provide ways for them to act effectively without doing damage to themselves or others. As adults, it is our responsibility to make schools safe for all students, but the reality is that most taunting and bullying that leads to harmful aggression occurs when educators are not present. Students need to learn that they have the power to decide who they will allow to influence them and who they won't. Since most conflict that students face with each other occurs when adults are not around (in the cafeteria, the hallways, the playground, or off school grounds after school), the activities in this chapter are designed to teach students skills and strategies to handle conflict effectively at these times. Therefore many of the activities are written directly for our students with prevention in mind. We want students to learn good decision-making strategies they can use when we are not around.

The activities are written so that students are led through the steps required for them to learn the skills and strategies. However, many of the strategies can be used after students have gotten into trouble to help them make a better decision next time. You will find an asterisk (*) next to those strategies that serve both purposes. You can adapt the directions to best fit your style and the needs within your classroom. To make these strategies most valuable, it is necessary to invest classroom time teaching them. It also helps for teachers to practice and model these strategies so that your own experience can be used as a guideline when teaching them to your students. Realize that all strategies work best when modeled with enthusiasm by the teacher. If you know of specific situations that occurred or are occurring, use these real events while teaching the strategies. Otherwise, ask your students what types of problem situations they or their classmates face and use them when teaching and practicing the strategies below.

Teach the six-step solution*

Note to educator: This six-step procedure can be learned and practiced by all students to give them an effective way of dealing with problem situations *before* they do something hurtful to themselves or others. The same steps can be used when processing a problem with one or more students. In the latter instance, we review the problem and poor decision made by the student that led to trouble by asking the student to consider whether or not he or she did all six of these steps. The six steps are

1. Stop and calm down.

2. Think.

3. Decide.

4. Choose a backup solution in case the first one doesn't work.

5. Act.

6. Evaluate.

After teaching the six-step solution, you might want to make a chart with the steps and hang it in your room. You'll also note that there are several questions to ask students in Steps 2, 3, and 6. We encourage you to create a master chart of the six steps and then individual charts that list each step along with relevant questions to write beneath. Now students can look at visual reminders while they are learning and internalizing these processes. Younger children might enjoy making art projects of each step.

Step 1: Stop and calm down. Before doing anything that we may feel sorry about later, the first thing to do is *stop. Do nothing.* There is always time to act on your first impulse later if that is what you decide to do. For some this is easier said than done.

When something happens that makes you mad, take a deep breath and picture a big red light or stop sign. Stopping gives you time to decide if the best thing to do is explode or if something else would be a better move.

Some students who are inclined to become confrontational quickly may have a hard time stopping. For them, another strategy, suggested by psychologist Dr. Kerry Gordon (2006), is to have them "turn in the opposite direction." He points out that our natural instincts physically move us toward the thing that is upsetting. By walking in the opposite direction, kids who need to move can still do so while getting away from the provocative stimulus.

Step 2: Think. After getting students to calm down, the next step is to teach them to think about the action they were about to take. An interesting thing happens every time you consider whether or not to do something. It gives you a chance to do something else! For example, if you are feeling mad because someone just called your mother a name and you get angry, that mad feeling may lead you to think, "I'll whop his a**." But as soon as you have that thought, there is a chance to do something else because you haven't done it yet. So after you stop and calm down, think before you decide and act.

Remind students that a major difference between humans and other animals is our ability to think and make choices. When animals are upset or under pressure, they either confront or run away from the problem (fight or flight). People often want to do those same things, and at times there are no better choices. Like other animals, we may still decide to run or fight, but at least we have done so after considering all the good and bad consequences.

Good thinking begins with good questions. Teach your students to ask these kinds of questions as a guide to making a good decision. It is important to see how the questions we ask ourselves lead to the decisions we want to have happen. They don't need to ask all of them, but it helps to know them so they can use the best ones, depending on the situation.

- Why am I feeling so mad or upset?
- Did I do anything that might have annoyed or offended the other person and caused his reaction? If so, what did I do?
- How does the other person feel?
- What is my problem?
- Who could I talk to about the problem before I do anything?
- Have I ever felt this way before?

- What did I do before to try to solve a similar problem?
- How did it work out?

Step 3: Decide. The next step is to actually make a decision. In making a decision, the two most important questions to ask yourself are

- What is my goal? (What do I want to have happen?)
- What are the possible consequences? (What will happen if I actually do what I think I should do?)

The first question asks students to choose a goal. All successful people have goals. This tells them what they want to achieve and when to feel proud of their accomplishment. The following are goals:

- I will do my homework for one hour.
- I will read two books and finish my book report two days before it is due.
- I will use the word *please* when I ask for something.
- I will use words rather than fists when I feel mad.

The second question asks students to think about likely consequences before doing something. For example, Paul calls Hector's mother a name. Hector's goal is to do something that gets Paul to stop while at the same time standing up to Paul so he doesn't look weak. Hector thinks, "I'll punch him in the face!" He quickly realizes that this solution might solve the problem because he won't look weak, but he also knows that Paul is pretty tough and might punch him back. He also knows that punching is against the rules and will likely lead to a suspension. Also, his guidance counselor will probably be disappointed if he gets into trouble again. Hector decides that Paul isn't worth the trouble, so he considers other options. Questions for him to ask himself are

- Will the solution I pick solve the problem?
- If I implement the solution, what might Paul do?

- Is the solution against the rules?
- What will other important people in my life do or think if I implement my solution?
- Am I willing to accept the consequences of the solution?

In this case, some of the solutions he considers are

- Punching him in the face
- Calling his mother a name
- Getting his friends after him
- Telling him to shut up
- Telling him I don't like what he said, I want him to stop, and that fighting is not worth it
- Looking him in the eye, saying nothing, and walking away
- Agreeing with him just to avoid a hassle because I know he is trying to get me in trouble
- Telling someone else to solicit other ideas

Each solution has consequences, so it is important that Hector consider the consequences before acting. He decides to walk away slowly and assertively by standing up straight and making brief eye contact. He makes this decision because even though he would like to punch Paul's lights out, he doesn't think Paul is worth the hassle of getting into trouble.

Step 4: Create a backup plan in case the first one doesn't work. Every sports team starts a game with a plan to beat the other team. If the plan works, they stay with it. But good coaches know that the plan may not work as well in the game as it did in practice. So before the game is even played, the coach and the team have a backup plan to use just in case. Just like a good coach, you need to have at least one more possible solution ready in case the first one doesn't work. You are your own coach!

Step 5: Act. Once you stop to calm down, think, decide, and create a backup plan, you have taken control of the situation. You are now in charge of what happens to you, so it is now time to act. It is time to carry out your decision to see if it works. You'll know it works if it meets your goal.

For example, when Hector decides to assertively walk away, he will soon know whether or not Paul stops or continues his put-downs. If he stops, then the solution worked. If he doesn't, then Hector either needs to give the solution more time to work or he needs to try a different solution. Some situations demand immediate action, and you'll want one or two solutions to use right away. If you have a recurring problem, you might want to try your first solution three or four times. If it's not working, then try another solution.

Step 6: Evaluate. The final three questions to ask in using this method are

1. Did I reach my goal?

2. If the same problem happens again, what will I do?

3. Are there any people I can think of (parents, friends, a teacher) who might help me figure out how to make my solution work or to help me think of another that might work better?

Practice the method

Give your students a scenario that is real or use the one below and have them practice using the six-step method.

Sally is in the cafeteria when she sees Lois and Joyce laughing and looking at her. They come closer and Lois says, "Where'd you get those clothes—at the Goodwill?" Both Lois and Joyce laugh even harder, and some of the other kids who are sitting nearby also hear this. Sally is embarrassed but doesn't know what to do. You are Sally's friend, and you want to help her deal with this situation. Help her decide on a solution by using the steps in the strategy above.

Successful students set and meet goals*

Goals are things that we want to achieve. We reach a goal by making a plan. If you are building a model airplane, directions help you assemble the model in the most precise way. A good plan helps you achieve your personal goals in the same way.

Setting goals helps you know when you have accomplished something of value. If using this strategy to review a choice with a student that led to a problem, start with the following:

- Decide on a goal that you want to reach and say it, then write it down. For example, "When someone bumps into me, I want to either walk away or say how I feel. I don't want to fight because I have decided that it isn't worth it. My goal is to . . ."
- When doing this with a student who got into trouble, ask if the student thinks the consequence was worth it.
- Decide on a plan you need to get you there. What are the steps you need to take in order to meet your goal (or not get into trouble again)? For example, "First, I'll walk far enough away so I probably won't bump into anyone. But if I do or they bump into me, I'll say, 'Excuse me.' If that isn't enough, I'll tell them I didn't mean anything by it—it was just an accident. If that still doesn't work, I'll tell them that getting into a fight isn't worth the hassle and then I'll get out of there as quickly as I can. If I'm still mad I might write my words down on a piece of paper and turn them into a poem that I can actually hand in to my teacher for credit or an extra credit grade."
  - Check your plan with a parent, teacher, or trusted friend.
  - Do each step in your plan, one step at a time.
- Reward yourself when you have reached your goal. Think about the things you enjoy. Pick something after you have accomplished your goal, and treat yourself for a job well done. You might even want to make a list of possible rewards and add to the list as you find new things. Keep the list handy as an easy reminder that your behavior has earned a reward.

There are many things we can control. Focus on those!

It is important for both teachers and students to understand the difference between problems they can solve and problems they can't. It is not always easy to tell the difference, but some things are obvious. You can control which television show you watch or which friend you call. You can't control whether the television works or whether your friend is interested in hanging out.

You can completely control some problems, but you cannot control all problems. We cannot control a parent's drinking problem, mom and dad's decision to divorce, or a father's choice to have no relationship with his child. As dependents, we don't control the neighborhood we live in or how much money our mother gets for child support. The idea is to figure out the problems in life over which we have some or complete control, and those over which we have no control. Then we can do something about the problems that can be solved or tell someone when we feel overwhelmed. We can also decide how to make the best of situations over which we have little control. By looking at things this way, we keep problems from growing so big that they consume our lives.

The first step is for us all (teachers and students) to write down things that make us angry. Next, we put a "C" next to those things over which we have a lot of control and we put an "N" next to those things over which we have no control. If you aren't sure, you might check with a trusted friend, teacher, counselor, or parent to get another opinion.

Next, set goals and develop plans to deal with those things over which you have control. For example, "I want to have more contact with my father (goal), so I will call him (plan)."

Decide what you will do if your plan doesn't work. For example, "I called my father, and he promised to pick me up for a visit but never came. He often lets me down. I'm going to invite him at least two more times for a visit, and if he doesn't come, I'm going to remind myself that he still loves me but that he has a lot of problems, and that my mother and grandmother love me, too." It can be helpful to figure this out with a trusted other person like a friend, parent, neighbor, or teacher. Sometimes school psychologists or social workers can help because they've received special training for helping students with these types of problems.

For the things on your list that have an "N" beside them, your challenge is to figure out how not to let them bother you as much as they are now. For example, "I can't control the fact that drugs are sold on the street corner and that lots of kids are shooting guns. I can control my decision to use guns if I ever have the opportunity or whether I should stay home late at night."

Practice the method

Read the following situation and then answer the questions below:

Jamil gets into fights at school. When that happens, he gets suspended. Some kids make fun of his clothes. Whenever someone calls him a name or says something nasty about his clothes or his family, he gets right into it with them by either calling the student a name or by hitting. Jamil's father almost never sees him. Jamil misses him a lot but doesn't tell anyone how he feels because he is embarrassed that his father has very little to do with him. A few older kids have tried to get Jamil to join their gang, and he is thinking about doing that. These gang kids are nice to him, they seem to have fun hanging out with each other, and Jamil is pretty lonely. His mom tries to get him to do his homework and talks to him about how important it is to do well in school. But Jamil doesn't always do his homework and says that he is bored at school. He doesn't like his teacher and she gets angry with him a lot because she thinks he doesn't try.

1. Does Jamil have any control over what his father does?

2. What do you think about his anger at other kids who call him names?

3. Is a fight with them worth the hassle of Jamil getting suspended from school?

4. How do you think Jamil really feels about his father?

5. It's tough on kids when their parents don't treat them right. Do you think that any of Jamil's anger that he gives to other kids really belongs to someone else?

6. What can Jamil do about his sadness that his father appears not to care so that he doesn't hurt himself by failing or by hurting others? What about his homework? Should he join the gang? Should he find other friends? Should he get help from anyone at school? What are the consequences of joining or not joining the gang, doing or not doing his homework, working or not working harder at school?

7. What advice would you give him to make good choices and handle whatever peer pressure he might face?

Solving my problems is not always easy, but it can be done*

Rather than get into trouble, here is better way to solve a problem. First, *name the problem.* Be specific in saying out loud what the problem is. It is not enough to say things like, "She's unfair!" "He doesn't like me!" "She's always getting on my case for no reason!" Those are too general. It is better to say, "She yells at me when she thinks I haven't worked hard enough." Or, "He bugs me when he thinks I'm bugging my little brother." Or, "The teacher and principal gave me detention because they saw me push another kid."

Next, *name what you want to have happen.* This is your goal. It may be something like, "I want the teacher to understand that math is hard for me, and even when I work hard I still usually don't understand," or "I want Mom to realize that my little brother doesn't listen when I talk," or "I want the teacher and principal to be fairer by knowing that the kid I pushed actually pushed me first."

Now, *say what you will do.* This is your plan. It may sound like, "I will tell the teacher that I need extra help because math is not my best subject," or, "I'll remind myself that pushing is against the rules even if I'm pushed first and that getting into trouble isn't worth it."

Next, *say what you will do if the plan doesn't work.* This is your backup plan. For example, "If the teacher doesn't give me extra help, I'll ask a friend or another teacher," or, "If the lock on my door is broken or my brother keeps banging, I'll turn up my radio," or, "If the kid keeps pushing me, I'll ask him to stop. Next I'll tell him to stop, and then finally tell whoever is in charge."

Next, tell your plan and backup plan *to someone you trust and respect for their feedback.* If there is nobody you choose to tell, ask yourself how you think someone you respect who usually solves problems peacefully would handle the situation.

Finally, *try your plan* at least three times. If things still don't work out, then try the backup plan at least three times. If that doesn't work, then talk it over to see if you can borrow an idea from someone you trust that may work better. So, if necessary, you might have to *change the plan.* Let's review:

Name the problem.

Name what you want to have happen.

Say what you will do.

Say what you will do if your plan does not work.

Check with someone you trust for his or her opinion.

Carry out your plan.

Change the plan if necessary.

Learn to handle frustration by becoming tolerant of others

All babies expect to have their needs met immediately. When hungry, they cry and expect to be fed. If they aren't fed, they keep crying. In a healthy, nurturing family, it is normal for them to be fed right away and totally sensible for them to get angry or scream if that doesn't happen.

As we grow and mature, we learn that we won't always have our needs met right away. We must learn that we cannot always eat or satisfy other bodily urges the instant we feel the need. It takes becoming mature to realize that not all people are nice or will treat us well all the time. Unless we realize that our needs will not always be met, we are doomed to feel frustrated or angry with other people for not giving us what we think we are entitled to. We may feel jealous of other people who have what we want or think we deserve. We must be willing to work for what we want and learn to accept that sometimes we'll get it and sometimes we won't.

Learning tolerance means practicing not feeling angry or frustrated when you don't get what you want. Here are some things to practice:

- If you are usually late to class every day, this week try to be late only twice.
- Say hello or good morning to a teacher you don't like, even if he or she doesn't reply.
- Walk away from someone trying to pick a fight with you.
- Ask another student for help before asking the teacher.
- Wait in line with a smile and positive thoughts.
- Raise your hand in class and wait to be recognized.
- Keep your cool when you think an adult in charge is being unfair (or treating you without equality).
- Work for 10 more minutes than usual on something you don't like to do.
- Work for 10 more minutes on something that you do like to make sure it is as good as you can possibly make it.
- Walk away if someone bumps you in the hall.
- Keep calm when someone cuts in front of you in line.
- Say something friendly to a kid you don't usually hang out with.

What situations have you seen that are good examples of times when students need to learn and practice tolerance? Learning tolerance doesn't happen overnight. It can be helpful when others appreciate the efforts we make to sacrifice things we want right away. Try noticing and appreciating other students or adults when you see them acting in a patient way. It can also help to keep a "Tolerance Journal" in which you record instances during the day when you wanted something right away but stayed calm and acted respectfully when it didn't work out the way you wanted it to.

Imagination can go a long way: The invisible shield or bulletproof vest*

Imagine owning a shield of steel armor or a bulletproof vest. When you have it on, nothing can penetrate it. The protection is so tough that swords bend and bullets ricochet. To be successful in the real world, each of us needs to build our own mental shield or vest so that we learn how not to let everything bother us. This kind of shield costs no money, and we can control when to use it.

First, recognize when someone is mentally attacking you. This is fairly easy to do. You know when someone is saying hurtful words, someone is in your face, or someone is saying negative things about you behind your back. Can you think of any other hurtful things that people do to make you feel mad? Be as specific as you can.

Next, picture your shield or bulletproof vest. Before you do anything about what is being said to or about you, picture putting on your shield or vest. What does it look like? If you had to draw it, could you? If not, keep working at it. It might even help to look at a book of ancient weapons to get some ideas for shields. Now that you are wearing your shield or vest, imagine that the attacker's words or looks are stopped by the vest or bent by the shield. You cannot be hurt as long as you are wearing the protection. Enjoy knowing that only you can see and feel the vest or shield. You can choose who you tell about it and who you don't.

Students who often blame others for their problems by claiming they only reacted to somebody else's provocation can often benefit by practicing this strategy. They learn they do not always have to react to trouble, even when somebody else is trying to get them into trouble.

Words are powerful and can get you into and out of trouble

Your invisible shield keeps you from being hurt during an attack, but you may need additional defenses if your opponents don't give up easily. For example, someone calls you or your mother a nasty name because he or she is determined to bait you into a fight. If you get into the fight (with your fists or words), chances are that things will only get worse: the police will be called, you will be suspended, you will be punished at home, and you might be hurt or even killed. Was it worth it? Maybe you think it was, but do you think that your mother would agree if you wound up hurt or dead?

Instead of fighting, you can learn to use safe words that will stop almost all attackers from continuing. At first, they will seem weird. You'll probably think that there is no way you could use these words because they aren't the real you. But with practice and discipline, you can keep others from robbing you of your self-control. Not all of the words will work all the time. But the more sentences you learn to use, the better prepared you will be to deal with the attack. It is very important that you practice these strategies so they eventually feel natural to use.

- Use "I" sentences. These are sentences that tell how you feel, what you want, and what you will do. They begin with the words "When you . . ." Then they tell the person how you feel: "I feel . . ." They end with telling the person what you want, expect, or will do. So there are three parts to an "I" sentence:

  When you (say or do) _____, I feel _____, and (or but) I want, will do, or expect _____.

For example, Jack takes Nancy's books. She says, "When you take my books I feel angry. I want my books back now."

José is bugged by Luis and Rolando to join their gang. He says, "When you ask me to join the gang, I feel honored because I know you think I'm tough. But I'm just interested in being friends with you guys."

Leo has just called Mitch's mom a nasty name. Mitch looks sternly at Leo and says, "When you call my mother that name, I get real upset and feel like busting you up. But getting into trouble isn't worth it, so I'm gonna walk away."

Practice the method

Let's give this a try. Imagine that someone is trying to get you into trouble. This person either said or did something that you don't like. Try to put your thoughts together and then use an "I" sentence.

- Be polite. Sometimes it works to use the word "please" as a way of getting someone to stop bugging you. For example, "Please give me my book back," or, "Please be careful. I don't like getting bumped."
- Agree with the put-down.* This requires a lot of self-confidence, but it can be an effective way to get someone to stop hassling, nagging, or bugging you. Learn to calmly agree with what the other person says. We know this is not easy because our normal reaction is to feel angry and to attack back. But when you attack back, you just wind up giving the person who bugged you what he or she wanted: power over you. After all, he or she was trying to get you mad, and by getting mad you are giving that person the control he or she wants. That just makes no sense.

Practice the method

Expect to practice this several times before you are ready to do it "for real." You have to do this without anger or sarcasm for it to work. Practice it several times before actually doing it in a real situation. Here are some practice examples:

- Stephie calls Mary a jerk. Mary says, "There may be some truth to that," while she walks away.

- Phillip takes Sam's hat and is teasing him. Four of Phillip's friends surround Sam. Sam says, "You must really like my hat. Either give it back when you're finished wearing it, or, if you really love it, I'll give it to you as a gift. See you later."
- Joy tells Lori that she has ugly teeth. Lori says, "I wish I had teeth as beautiful as yours. They're really white and pretty."

Encourage your students to practice agreeing when someone is trying to get them mad or in trouble. It is very difficult to do but often terrifically effective. In particular, students who impulsively react when their buttons are pushed can gain a very effective tool that can help them avoid trouble.

Try to understand*

There may be some good reasons that you don't understand when someone tries to pick a fight. Maybe if you understood things better, you would be better able to say or do the right thing. When someone is coming at you and you aren't sure why, try saying something like, "I must have really done something to make you feel mad. What did I do? I sure would like you to tell me so that I won't make the same mistake again." Or, "Wow, you look mad. When you calm down please tell me why you are so upset so I'll know how to fix my mistake. See you later."

Apologize

It takes a lot of guts to recognize when you have done something wrong and own up to the problem. Put yourself in someone else's shoes. Ask how you would feel if someone said or did the same thing to you that you just said or did to someone else. When you realize you did something wrong, be tough enough to go to that person and apologize. When said with meaning, the words, "I'm sorry" go a long way toward helping settle a problem so that no violence occurs. You can even apologize when you aren't sure that you did anything wrong but someone is really mad at you. At those times you might say something like, "I'm sorry if I did something that made you mad. I didn't mean to upset you."

Put the blame on someone else

Imagine three guys see Bob walking home. They come over and show him cocaine, weed, or uppers. The pressure is on. They make him feel that to belong to their group or even feel safe he has to join them, but he really doesn't want to. Bob is quick on his feet and remembers that his Mom told him that he can always blame her when he doesn't want to join the group but is afraid of what might happen. He says, "Wow, I'd love to join you, but if I don't get home right away, my mom is gonna kill me!" Another possibility is for Bob to say something like, "I'd love to (name the problem you want to avoid), but I'd (make an excuse) so (tell what you will do)." Here are two examples.

- Steve is pressuring Jim to steal. Jim says, "Man, I'd love to own that stuff, but seeing how I'm always dropping things I'd just mess you up. Thanks for asking but I'd better stick to stuff I'm good at."
- Laticia, Josie, and Ellen ask Lisa to party with them. Lisa knows that alcohol is going to be there, and so are some guys who pressure girls to have sex. She isn't interested but doesn't want to look like a geek. She says, "I'd love to have a good time, but I gotta look after my little brother tonight or my Mom is gonna be mad and I'm gonna be grounded forever. Have a good time."

Practice the method

Who in your life can you blame (for cover) so that you can avoid embarrassment in front of friends while making it clear that something terrible will happen to you if you join them? Name a situation with others in which you don't want to be involved but would be worried about what others would think if you were honest. Practice saying something that blames your cover person so that you can avoid the uncomfortable situation and still save face.

Release frustration by
writing letters or keeping a journal

When you are really angry, it is important to find ways of letting off steam. It can help to write down all of your thoughts and feelings in a letter or a journal. Most people choose to keep this information private, but there are times when you might even share this writing with the people who made you feel mad. You'll need to decide whether there is any benefit to sharing these thoughts or whether it is just better to write them down and keep them to yourself. We have found that it is usually best to wait at least one or two days after writing the letter to decide whether or not there is any good reason to send it. That gives us time to calm down and use our heads rather than just our impulses.

Imagine that Raja teases Chen about his clothes and hairstyle. Chen feels mad, and his first thought is to tease back. But he remembers that Raja and his friends are usually looking for trouble. He decides there is a good chance that if he gets into it with Raja, the problems will only get worse. But he is steaming and feels like belting Raja. He decides to write a note in his private journal: "I can't stand stupid Raja. What a jerk! I would really like to rip his head off or just scream obscenities at him. But if I did, the jerk would probably get his friends after me and I don't need that kind of trouble. So I'm telling you, my friend, rather than him."

For students who often get into trouble, it can be helpful for them to learn alternative ways to express their feelings. Some can write while others can draw or talk to a trusted friend or adult.

Take responsibility for the school:
it's everyone's job

At one high school in the Los Angeles area, teachers encourage students to take responsibility by letting them know that it is okay for them to tell on classmates who are breaking laws. At this school, students are actually given reward money for turning over the names of students who carry weapons, destroy school property, take things that belong to others, and deface school grounds with graffiti. The reward money is given when adults find that the student who was named actually did the misdeed. In that school, care is taken to make sure that if one student tells on another, it is done in such a way that the student who broke the rules doesn't know who did the telling. That way, nobody has to worry about somebody wanting to get even.

Not everyone agrees that giving money rewards is a good idea, but most think it is great when the school is safe for everyone. Sometimes there just aren't enough hall monitors, principals, or teachers to make the school safe. Together, students can make a huge difference in how things are at their school. It is important that they are encouraged to find safe and effective ways to watch out for each other. The following questions are designed to get students thinking about how they can make their school a safer place:

1. Are there things that make you feel unsafe at school?

2. Are there things at your school that don't make you feel unsafe but you think make others feel unsafe?

3. Are there rules at your school that are supposed to protect you from the things that are happening in the first two questions?

4. If you know that there are rules or laws that are supposed to keep others from doing these things, why do you think these things happen anyway?

5. What responsibilities do you think students should have for safety at the school?

6. What things do you think you or others might do that can help send a message to the kids who do dangerous or hurtful stuff at school?

7. How do you think adults at your school would react if they received an unsigned note from someone like you

telling about something dangerous that someone did or was about to do?

8. What do you think about the idea of rewarding students for telling on other students who are breaking laws and making the school less safe?

9. What plan do you think students should follow if they find out about possible dangers at school? Outside of school?

KEY POINTS FROM THE CHAPTER

Teachers often assume that their students have the skills and tools necessary to defuse potentially explosive situations. We believe that these skills need to be taught. The six-step procedure can be learned and practiced by all students to give them an effective way of dealing with problem situations before they do something hurtful to themselves or to others.

It is important to take real class time to teach these responses. Some teachers even test or quiz their students on how well they are able to defuse practice scenario situations in class. Writing things down can be a great release of stress and energy. We recently met a teacher who encourages students to write as much poetry as they can. She points out that rap stars such as Eminem, Snoop Dogg, and 50 Cent are actually poets, who are successful because they write down their feelings instead of acting on them.

When students learn real defusing techniques their lives become easier. They no longer have to worry about peer pressure or looking tough in front of each other. This is probably the hardest set of skills for kids to develop. Teaching them requires patience, practice, and dedication. The rewards are well worth it.

9

Helping Students Handle Bullying

Bullying is a special form of aggression in which there is an imbalance in power between the bully and the victim. Bullies generally feel no power in any part of their lives outside of school, so they find a victim to pick on, which allows them to feel in control. Most strategies in Chapter 8 can help students feel sufficiently empowered so that they don't need to be the bully or the victim. This chapter offers ideas, strategies, and suggestions that can help deal effectively with this specific issue.

Most of the strategies below will help with traditional bullying situations that happen in school. However, more recently, a new form of high-tech bullying has emerged. It is called cyber-bullying and is now the most popular form of bullying among kids. Victims are no longer safe when they go home, and can feel tormented 24 hours a day. School personnel, students, and parents all must play a role in helping solve this problem. Teachers and parents need to educate themselves when it comes to technology. Too many teachers just "call the tech guy" when something is wrong with the computer system. Many parents view the computer as a place to "check their e-mail" every now and then. With better under-standing comes a better chance of helping make this problem disappear.

Cyber-bullying involves the use of information and tech-nologies such as e-mail, cell phones, and pager text messages. The causes of cyber-bullying are usually the same as school bullying, with power, control, and intimidation at the root. Sadly, however, there often is no one there to stop it and the victim is no longer able to go home to get away from the taunts and threats. The statistics related to this form of bully-ing are startling. More than 55 percent of students said that someone had said hurtful or angry things to them online. Thirty-five percent of students say they have been threatened online by another student (Keith & Martin, 2005). Web sites are also commonly used by bullies to spread hateful mes-sages, post nasty pictures, and torment others. In New York City, a group of students created a Web site to determine who was the biggest "ho" in their school. It took a call from the Brooklyn district attorney to have the site shut down (Keith & Martin, 2005).

Students are also using technology to take pictures of fights on their camera phones and of unsuspecting peers in locker rooms. Some even have the capability of sending videos to one another. Students, parents, and staff all need to learn how to help defeat the bullies so our schools can be safe places for learning to occur for all.

Here are a few specific suggestions for how teachers can help their students that are victimized by this type of bullying:

Help students who are victims of cyber-bullying

Do not reply or respond to text messaging, video messag-ing, or e-mails that are obscene, abusive, or vulgar. Remember, whoever is sending them is seeking a response. Do not give them that satisfaction. This is hard to do, but it is essential in getting the bullying to stop.

Most chat rooms allow people to be whomever they want. This can help if you are a victim. Set up an alias that doesn't give out any information about your age, gender, or location. Then give your new screen name to only a few of your closest friends.

Do not delete obscene or abusive e-mails or text messages. The natural reaction will be to delete them because of how nasty they are. However, all messages are stamped with date and time. Most can be traced to the computer from which they were sent. Also, many states are passing laws making cyber-bullying illegal. It is recommended to either save or print the messages. They can be used as evidence if legal action becomes necessary.

Tell trusted adults about what has happened, and encourage them to call the police. If there are threats associated with the messages, do not be afraid to get the police involved. Sometimes the presence of the police alone will get the bully to change his or her ways. It is usually good to try to allow students to handle problems on their own. However, when the relentless attacks do not stop, getting an adult and/or the police involved can really help.

Offer parents suggestions for their cyber-bullied kids

At Oak View Elementary School in Fairfax County, Virginia, a student decided to do a survey on the top five "hated kids" in the sixth grade. He set up a Web site where kids could vote for their least favorites. Students were voted off until only one remained as the most hated. The parents of the "most-hated kid" showed up at the school saying their daughter was refusing to attend because of the humiliation that she faced (Lisante, 2005). Unfortunately, most parents of bullies do not want to believe that their son or daughter harasses others. Many parents of victims are not sure what to do, and occasionally believe the bullying will get worse if they intervene. Here are some suggestions teachers can give to parents:

Contact the school and let them know what is going on. Most schools take this type of bullying very seriously and have a process in place for helping both the victim and the student.

Contact your Internet service provider. This can give you information about who is doing the bullying, where it is coming from, and the time of day it is happening. Almost all providers have some form of parental controls. America On-Line has the "AOL Guardian," which reports who kids exchange messages with and what Web sites they visit. They also have monitored chat rooms for children 13 years and under and an instant messaging "safe list" that restricts who children can talk with. Yahoo and Microsoft have similar programs. Yahoo even offers a weekly "report card" of a child's online activity during the prior week.

Keep computers in a public room. Kids are less likely to harass each other when they know an adult might see. By keeping the computer in a public room, parents can check in on children to make sure they are using the technology in an appropriate way.

Press charges. Some parents are afraid to press charges because they think the bullying might get worse. Bullies must be confronted, and pressing charges sends a clear message that "bullying is not okay and will not be accepted."

Teachers and schools can prevent bullying

Most schools focus on intervention when it comes to bullying. They try to get it to stop by working with the victims and the bullies. We will address intervention in this chapter. However, more important than intervention is prevention. The goal really should be to get kids to like each other and to want to be around each other. Much of what schools do on a daily basis actually causes bullying. If you really want it to stop bullying, here are a few things to do immediately:

Preventing bullying begins with getting kids to like each other. One way to do this is to reward your entire class in honor of a student or a group of students. For example, you could say, "Because Jenny has behaved herself all week and I am so proud of her, you all get an extra 15 minutes on the playground in honor of Jenny. Do not thank me, thank her!" By rewarding everyone in Jenny's honor, all students feel good about Jenny's accomplishment. When on the playground they might even thank her for her outstanding behavior. Some might even say, "Way to go, Jenny. You better be good again next week!" Schools can do the same thing. Instead of having a "National Honor Society Breakfast," have a breakfast for the entire school in honor of the National Honor Society kids. Now all students get a chance to eat and no one is singled out.

Stop publicly rewarding individual students. Every time a teacher rewards an individual student in public, most other students get annoyed with the individual being rewarded. In the above example, if the teacher chooses to reward only Jenny for her good behavior, other students will complain that "they are always good and they don't get extra time on the playground!" They will begin to resent Jenny, which might lead to name calling and aggression. Many teachers think that if they give a student a ticket, point, or sticker, it motivates others to want that as well. In fact, the opposite is true. Difficult and disruptive students do not try to be more like the rewarded student. Instead they say, "Whatever with him or her. She always gets everything. I can't stand her." These feelings lead to resentment, which often leads to bullying.

Eliminate class rankings, valedictorians, and salutatorians: The reason for this is simple. If one student is often ranked first and another is often ranked last, the student at the bottom begins to dislike the student at the top. The student at the bottom then gets others near the bottom to dislike those at the top as well. They might even begin calling each other names. A divisiveness builds that often leads to name calling and physical altercations. In addition to the divisiveness, ranking students against each other fosters a competitive environment among those at the top. Often kids will not push themselves to take more advanced classes for fear their ranking will slip. Students are less likely to help each other because one might not want another to overtake his or her ranking. Kids at the top know they are good. They don't need to be ranked. Those at the bottom only feel bad when they see how poorly they measure against those at the top.

Integrate curriculum-based anti-bullying programs into classrooms. Counselors, social workers, and psychologists all can play a part in these programs. Some schools will bring in guest speakers, including respected community leaders and officials, to talk about the harm bullying can do.

Start early. From the time students enter school, they should be educated and taught about cyber-bullying and the negative effects it has on other kids. Begin showing them how to use a computer at an early age. This is also the time to teach about how not to hurt others while using the computer.

Update all policies, handbooks, and rules to include a ban on cyber-bullying. Be sure to publicly let students know how seriously you take cyber-bullying. Let them know up front that it will generate the same punishment as in-school bullying or fighting. Some students believe that if it happens away from school, there is nothing the school can do. This is not true, and we must tell our students as much.

Figure out who the bullies are and why they are bullying. It takes a lot of work to change a bully's attitude. They are usually seeking power and control. If schools can recognize this, they have a chance to put the bully in a position of power in a positive way. There are numerous suggestions for how to do that in previous chapters.

Teachers and schools can handle traditional bullying

In addition to protecting our students, it is necessary to help them learn how to handle themselves during difficult moments with each other and in tough situations when adults are not around to intervene. We can help kids know what to do and how to do it by understanding bullies and teaching the victim specific things to do in order to get the bullying to stop. In her book, *The Bully, the Bullied, and the Bystander*, Barbara Coloroso (2002) breaks bullying down into three categories: every member of the situation is either a bully, a person being bullied, or a bystander.

Strategies for working with the victim

A few years back I (BDM) had a boy named Teddy in my fourth-grade class. He was often withdrawn and sad. Teddy was quite small for his age and struggled both socially and academically. I noticed he didn't have many friends and would sometimes sleep in class. As I got to know Teddy, I paid particular attention to his behavior near the times he left my room for lunch, gym, music, or art. Before lunch I often noticed Teddy become upset. Finally, one day he told me he hated going to lunch because Bobby always picked on him, called him names, and threatened to take his money. I was shocked to hear Bobby mentioned as a bully. This was one of my favorite students. A hard worker, polite, and popular, Bobby was the last student I thought of as a bully. Later, I learned that bullies can be excellent con artists. Often they appear to be sweet, friendly, and kind, but have the ability to switch gears when nobody is watching.

I asked Teddy to eat lunch in class with me that day. I told him I wanted to discuss the situation he was having with Bobby when no one else was around. After getting his lunch Teddy came in the room upset. He looked at me and said he was terrified that I would say something and things would get worse. I assured him I would let him handle it on his own, for now. I then asked Teddy to tell me some of the things Bobby said to him. It was the classic, "your Mama" stuff, and a few other things. Teddy said that the worst thing Bobby called his mama was a "stupid ho." In the previous section, I talked about power, and about not having it taken away. Here is an example of how to convince Teddy his power was being taken away. The rest of our conversation went like this:

Mr. M: Wow, that really isn't nice. Teddy, do you know that when Bobby says stuff like that he is trying to take away all of your power? Do you know what that means?

Teddy: No.

Mr. M: He wants you to get mad, upset, and react. When you give him what he wants he is in complete control of you. So, do you want to give him all of your power that easily?

Teddy: No. But it is upsetting when he says stuff like that in front of other kids.

Mr. M: I know. But for a few minutes I want you to try something. Let's just imagine that instead of calling your mom a "stupid ho" he said "Teddy, your mom is a 'smart lady.'"

Teddy: *(with a slight smile)* I wish he would say that. My mom is really smart.

Mr. M: I know she is. So next time he calls your mom a name I want you to imagine he said what I did and I want you to respond the way you did. By laughing.

Teddy: That's gonna be hard.

Mr. M: I know. But Teddy, are you telling me all anyone has to do to make you mad is change two words? Because all we did was change two words and you went from being mad to laughing!

Teddy: I never thought of it that way. Okay. I'll try it.

Mr. M: You try it. I'm going to have a little conversation with Bobby as well. Don't worry though, I promise I will be sure to make it seem like you had nothing to do with me talking to him.

It is important to show victims how they may be unwittingly contributing to the bullying. It is not the victim's fault, and we don't want to portray that. However, it is good to show them how the bully often takes power away easily. It is also good to show them a few things they might do to make them less likely to be victimized.

This is true for teachers, as well. In seminars, we sometimes do an activity in which they ask teachers if they have ever been "flipped off" by a student (having the middle finger raised). Many acknowledge that this has happened at least a time or two. We then ask the group how the middle finger made them feel. The answers range from outrage to shock. We then stick up our thumbs at the group and ask how they would feel if somebody tried to "flip them off" with the thumb. Most in attendance laugh. The feelings are obviously much different. The next question is, "Are you telling us that all we have to do is change one finger and we can take away all your power? Amazing what a difference a digit can make in changing an attitude, thought, and feeling!" Explain this concept to victims. When they understand it, this can be a strong thought process for them when they are in the moment of an in-school bullying situation.

It is not unusual for victims to be uninvolved in extracurricular school activities. They often don't play sports, aren't involved in any clubs or activities, and usually have no real outward interests. Part of our job is to get them involved. For example, if a student likes to draw, we might see if they can go to the art room or join art club. Another idea is helping them get involved with self-defense or mixed martial arts training, which accomplishes two important goals: First, it involves the student in an activity that builds self-confidence and gives the student a way to defend himself or herself. Second, it can be an avenue for the student to make friends. Remember, activities create involvement, and involvement usually leads to friends and self-confidence. The victim will eventually be seen as a person with talents and abilities just like everyone else. It is our job to steer them in the right direction.

Strategies for working with the bully

Working with the bully is usually more complex than working with the victim. Almost always, the victim wants help and is eager for ideas and advice. The bully does not. Bullies deny doing anything wrong, and if that doesn't work, they often promise to stop immediately. Earlier in this book, we discussed the importance of getting to the root of disruptive behavior. This also is true when it comes to bullying. If our only goal is to stop the bullying, we will not really help the bully, and probably the bully will continue the destructive pattern when adults are not around. Of course we want the bullying to stop, but that should not be good enough. We want the attitude to change, too. Here are three major reasons kids bully each other:

They are bullied outside of school by a parent or sibling. It is all they know.

They are seeking attention from the other kids.

They are seeking power and control because outside of school they have neither.

It is not uncommon to learn that a bully is being abused mentally, physically, or both, at home. People who should love and care about them have victimized them. Occasionally they are encouraged by older siblings or parents to be "in charge" on the playground or the lunchroom. They are taught that the tougher they seem the more respect they will earn. Sometimes these kids will go home and brag that they beat someone up or that everyone is afraid of them. Approval and praise for these acts, although sometimes subtle, is not uncommon.

Begin to view the bully as you would your own child. A good trusting relationship is important. Bullies, too, need to have complete confidence and belief in us that they can discuss their home lives in a noncritical and nonjudgmental way. This relationship can begin by asking the child what he or she does after school and at home.

In many of our other books, we have shared a strategy called the "2 by 10" that can be very helpful in working with bullies. The "2" stands for two uninterrupted minutes per day. The "10" stands for ten consecutive days. Our goal during these two minutes is to have a conversation with the student about anything other than school. You may often find that during the first few days students usually share very little. They will put their heads down, roll their eyes, and perhaps even grunt or snort. Do not fear. Eventually the student will begin conversing with you. This is an excellent path to making a personal connection. Occasionally, they acknowledge verbal or physical abuse outside of school, which enables them to see how their behavior toward others in school is no better. This is a difficult conversation to have. The goal is two consecutive minutes of conversation, but at the beginning one minute might be enough. The conversation should happen in the most private place we can find.

As teachers, our instinctive reaction when we hear about bullying is to bully the bullies. We often scold, tell them to stop, and threaten punitive actions. This occasionally gets them to stop for a brief period of time, but almost never changes the behavior long term. We must get to a place where the student trusts us enough to listen to what we say. Educators can then praise the bully when he or she is making good choices. These students need to know that we will notice them just as often when they are doing the right thing as we do when they are doing the wrong thing.

Threatening to get parents involved does not usually generate long-term change. However, occasional phone calls home to praise a bully's "leadership qualities" can be helpful, which may enable you to more effectively engage parental cooperation at a later time.

As mentioned earlier, attention, power, and control are often at the root of bullying. In the bully's eyes other kids look up to him, they respect him, and as a result he has a sense of his own value and worth. Teachers often show these students the attention they crave. They have private conversations asking the bully to stop. They discuss the student at faculty meetings and in the staff lunchroom. It is not uncommon for the bully to become the most popular topic among faculty. We must combat this by showing the student attention and giving him power and control in other ways. This student should be our group leader. He needs to be put in charge of things we value that can benefit others.

Dean Likner, a teacher in San Diego, put his bully, Chris, in charge of playground safety. He also made him the bully monitor. He told Chris that he was in charge of looking out for bullying situations and for making sure they didn't happen. More important, Chris was trusted to help get the bullying behaviors to stop in a nonviolent way. Mr. Likner kept an eye on the playground and made sure Chris was doing his job. After every recess Mr. Likner met privately with Chris to assess how things were going on the playground. The better things got, the more responsibility and praise Chris received. Bullying and aggression on the playground decreased with Chris in charge.

Remember, working with bullies is worth it. They may even become the best leaders we have. Once they are on our side, we can persuade an unruly, out-of-control class to settle down.

Strategies for working with the bystanders

A bystander is anyone other than the bully or the victim. Bystanders often include other students, teachers, administrators, and support personnel. Bystanders play a large role in the bullying process, because without them, bullying behavior would almost never happen. Just as there is almost always an audience for a fight, bullies do most of their damage in the presence of other students.

Bystanders take on one of three roles. The first group joins the bully and helps torment the victim. Without the bully they could be influenced by someone else, possibly in a positive way. This is the most important group of bystanders to reach. They have asserted some power by siding with the bully. However, a strong teacher who is also a leader can convince this group that the bully is just using them. This type of bystander can be convinced that true power is had by not joining the bully. It is possible to get family support from this group. We have no problem calling parents and telling them that their child is making some bad decisions by siding with the school bully who is tormenting a peer. In directly working with bystanders, the first goal is to get these kids to stop following the bully. Most people don't like to view themselves as followers. This is why it is okay to tell students when you think they are. Be sure to tell them exactly and specifically why you think they are followers. Often they will respond by saying, "I'm not a follower!" This is the perfect time to tell them, "Good, then stop doing whatever 'Chris' says or does when you are on the playground!" An effective intervention is to have consequences for bystanders or onlookers. When they know there is a cost to them for being in the presence of bullying, finding another place to be becomes more attractive.

A second goal is to encourage bystanders to help influence the bully in other ways. This part can be difficult, because the bully often has asserted his power over the others. But once this group of bystanders is no longer joining in, they will begin to do other things and get involved with other kids. There is strength in numbers. This alone can be enough to get a bully to stop.

The majority of students watch silently, fearing that if they help the victim they will draw attention to themselves and be the next victim. Most of these kids hate the bully but are afraid to do or say anything. When rallied by a good leader they can have a lot of influence. It is important to know who, specifically, is in this group and to meet with them privately. Explain that you understand their concerns about becoming a victim, but that together they have a very strong voice and, more important, they have each other. They need to understand that it is their school and that they have full support of the teacher, principal, and all other school personnel in the building. We must attempt to get this group of kids to include the victim in their games and activities. A student in a group is much more difficult to pick on than a student who is alone. All students can be trained to support the victim when they see bullying occur. For example, students can learn to say to the victim, "You don't need to listen to that. Let's go." And leaders can remind bullies, "We don't do that here."

The final and rarest of the three groups of bystanders are the victim defenders. In some schools and situations this group does not even exist. In others there are one or two students willing to help. Unfortunately, this group can easily be overpowered by the bully and his followers. The defenders help for a short period of time, but eventually wilt away under the pressure. They usually begin withdrawing from the victim and wind up joining one of the other two groups. This is even worse for the victim, because he or she gets a brief taste of what friendship is like before it is ripped away. The defenders must be recognized immediately and strongly supported by the school. We must get onlookers to help the defenders by forming their own larger group. The bigger picture is developing a school culture where bullying and what to do about it is taught so that all recognize when it occurs. All can then be empowered to prevent it through inclusion of peers, and safely confront it when seen. Much work and effort is required. Just as bullies were not built overnight, they will not be changed overnight. Nevertheless, much can be done to deal with this difficult issue.

KEY POINTS FROM THE CHAPTER

Do your best to get kids liking each other. This is so important to building a positive environment in a classroom. Compare student work to their own previous work. Send the message that says, "I need you to behave better today than you did yesterday. You don't necessarily need to be as good as others in the class, but you have to be better today than you were yesterday!" When kids compete against themselves they always have a chance to succeed. Even the student who is functioning at the lowest level in the class can accomplish the goal of doing one more math problem today than the student did yesterday.

To get bullying to really stop will require many schools to make drastic changes. Save the competitive environments for the football field, basketball court, and baseball diamond. Classrooms should be inviting, warm places. They can't be this way if students are forced to compete against each other. Remember to reward your entire class in honor of a student or a group of students. This will go a long way in fostering a positive learning environment.

Conclusion

After a recent seminar in Canada, Mr. Hughes, the sponsor, was driving me (ANM) to the airport when he shared a story about one of his former students. He told me that he knew Cory, a boy who was both deeply troubled and somewhat cognitively challenged, throughout his high school years. In the role of assistant principal, Mr. Hughes was often required to give his attention to Cory for one behavior or another. Mr. Hughes shared how, for reasons not entirely clear, Cory was one of those kids who not only saw him when he was in trouble, but sought him out just to talk and be with. In his junior year of high school, shortly after Easter, Cory showed Mr. Hughes the gift his mother had given him for the holiday: five $100 bills placed inside a card. The card read, "To Cory: Happy Easter. I hope I never see your f***ing face again." It was his mother's parting gesture as she marched off into the sunset with her abusive boyfriend.

Sadly, stories like Cory's have become more normal than exceptional in some schools. Not uncommon is for caring adults like teachers to become numb and insensitive to these harsh realities, because to confront and recognize them on a regular basis is to require a major paradigm shift from "get them to achieve standards" to "nurture their humanity." Yet with children experiencing major life crises on nearly a daily basis, we must reframe our concept of the classroom to include affirmation of them and validation of their real-life experiences. We may not be able to do everything for everybody, but we can at least do a little bit for each person. Harmful student behavior is no accident. Frequently, it is an

149

expression of the pain and torment visited too often on those unequipped to handle them by those who are supposed to care. It is often the little caring human gestures: a smile, a listening ear, a handshake, greeting, or hug, that can so meaningfully change a life. How often do we struggle with students who drive us up the wall all year, only to be visited years later by that same student who tells us we were his or her favorite teacher? We never know the effect educators have on students, especially the effect caring, nurturing teachers have. Students who are difficult, disruptive, or uncooperative almost never thank you for the effort and energy you put into them on a daily basis.

When I asked Mr. Hughes what happened to Cory, he told me that Cory's life has been anything but smooth, but he is gainfully employed, married, and a loving father.

We hope that you have found and will continue to find the information and strategies in this book helpful for knowing what to do and how to respond when your students with the most challenging behaviors push your buttons. On behalf of all of your "Cory's," thank you for the gifts of your time, patience, caring, and determined effort to matter in their lives and to turn our schools into safer, more caring homes away from home for all children.

References

Asimov, N. (2005, March 24). Report blasts state over dropouts: Graduation rates inflated, study finds. *San Francisco Chronicle*. http://sfgate.com/cgi-bin/article.cgi?file=/c/a/2005/03/24/MNGPUBU2811.DTL.

Children's Defense Fund. (2005). 2005 gun report. http://www.childrensdefense.org/site/PageServer?pagename=education_gun violence_gunreport2005_default.

Coloroso, B. (2002). *The bully, the bullied and the bystander*. Toronto, Ontario, Canada: HarperCollins.

Curwin, R., & Mendler, A. (1988). *Discipline with dignity*. Alexandria VA: Association for Supervision and Curriculum Development.

Curwin, R., & Mendler, A. (1999). *Discipline with dignity*. Alexandria VA: Association for Supervision and Curriculum Development (Original work published 1988).

Gardner, H. (1983). *Frames of mind: The theory of multiple intelligences*. New York: Basic Books.

Gardner, H. (1999). *The disciplined mind: Beyond facts and standardized tests: The K–12 education that every child deserves*. New York: Simon & Schuster.

Herr, N. (2005). Television & health. *The sourcebook for teaching science*. Retrieved October 2, 2006, from http://www.csun.edu/science/health/docs/tv&health.html.

Keith, S., & Martin, M. (2005). Cyber-bullying: Creating a culture of respect in a cyber world. *Reclaiming Children and Youth, 13*(4), 224.

Larsen, E. (2003). Violence in U.S. public schools: A summary of findings. *Institute of Education Sciences, 4*.

Lavoie, R. (Producer), (1989). *How difficult can this be? F.A.T. City workshop*. [Video]. (Available at http://www.ricklavoie.com)

Lisante, J. (2005). Cyber bullying: No muscles needed. Retrieved October 1, 2006, from www.connectforkids.org.

Marzano, R. J. (2003). *What works in schools: Translating research into action*. Alexandria, VA: Association for Supervision and Curriculum Development.

Mendler, A. (1997). *Power struggles: Successful techniques for educators.* Rochester, NY: Discipline Associates.

Mendler, A. (2005). *Just in time: Powerful strategies to promote positive behavior.* Bloomington, IN: National Education Service.

Robinson, C., & Kakela, P. (2006). Creating a space to learn: A classroom of fun, interaction, and trust. *College Teaching, 54*(1).

Tomlinson, C. A. (2005). Traveling the road to differentiation in staff development. *Journal of Staff Development, 26*(4).

Walls, C. (2003). *Providing highly mobile students with an effective education.* ERIC Clearinghouse on Urban Education.

Yaussi, S. (2004). Interview with Salome Thomas-El: Principal, teacher, and chess coach. *The Clearing House, 77*(6), 269.

Index

CORWIN PRESS

The Corwin Press logo—a raven striding across an open book—represents the union of courage and learning. Corwin Press is committed to improving education for all learners by publishing books and other professional development resources for those serving the field of PreK–12 education. By providing practical, hands-on materials, Corwin Press continues to carry out the promise of its motto: **"Helping Educators Do Their Work Better."**